Literary Criticism in Perspective
Robert Bly: The Poet and His Critics

About *Literary Criticism in Perspective*

Books in the series *Literary Criticism in Perspective* trace literary scholarship and criticism on major and neglected writers alike, or on a single major work, a group of writers, a literary school or movement. In so doing the authors — authorities on the topic in question who are also well-versed in the principles and history of literary criticism — address a readership consisting of scholars, students of literature at the graduate and undergraduate level, and the general reader. One of the primary purposes of the series is to illuminate the nature of literary criticism itself, to gauge the influence of social and historic currents on aesthetic judgments once thought objective and normative.

Robert Bly:
The Poet and His Critics

William V. Davis

Robert Bly:
The Poet and His Critics

C A M D E N   H O U S E

PUBLISHED BY CAMDEN HOUSE, INC.
DRAWER 2025
COLUMBIA, SC 29202 USA

Printed on acid-free paper.
Binding materials are chosen for strength and
durability.

ISBN:1-879751-79-8

Library of Congress Cataloging-in-Publication Data

Davis, William Virgil, 1940-
     Robert Bly : the poet and his critics / William V. Davis.
          p.   cm.   -- (Studies in English and American Literature, Linguistics,
          and culture)
     Includes bibliographical references (p. 83) and index.
     1. Bly, Robert--Criticism and interpretation--History. Il. Title.
     II. Series.
     PS3552.L9Z637   1994
     811'.54--dc20   93-38308
                                                                                CIP

Contents

To
Robert Bly
and to all his critics
and
to my wife
Carol
and to our son
Bill

for the time these words have taken

Introduction

ALL LITERARY CRITICISM FACES THE CHALLENGE of the future, just as all writers do, but an account of the literary criticism of a contemporary writer is unique. Although there are often fewer of the writer's works to consider, they are frequently hard to find, and they are difficult to evaluate objectively since there is so little time between them and the criticism. If the writer in question is still active, controversial, and prolific in a variety of genres, his career still in progress, the challenge is even greater.

The other problem in dealing with a contemporary writer whose career and canon are still far from complete is that there are fewer critical materials available for the most immediately recent works since the critical canon takes such a long time to grow up around literary works. Also, many critics shy away from contemporary works or are not willing or able to commit themselves in any definitive way before some inkling of the historical judgment has at least begun to be made. Therefore, in many instances, all that is available on the latest works are the early reviews.

Thus, in a study such as this one, it is inevitable that the most recent works remain the least covered critically, though they may prove to be the most important works. Obviously, then, this study of the history of the criticism of Bly's work to date is a work in progress, just as Bly's career and his canon are still in progress.

Robert Bly was born in 1926 in the small town of Madison, Minnesota. He attended a one-room school, then, after graduation from the local high school, enlisted in the Navy. He became interested in poetry during his military service and, after being discharged from the service, attended St. Olaf's College for one year, and then transferred to Harvard. There, he quickly joined a literary circle that included fellow students Richard Wilbur, John Ashbery, Frank O'Hara, Kenneth Koch, and Donald Hall.[1] Bly became literary editor of the Harvard *Advocate* in his junior year, won the Garrison Prize for Poetry in his senior year, and wrote the class poem for his *magna cum laude* graduation in 1950.

Having chosen to make his career as a poet and feeling "an instinct" for solitude, Bly isolated himself in New York City for several years after he graduated from college, reading and writing on his own. In 1954 he enrolled in the creative writing program at the University of Iowa and completed a collection of poems as his M. A. thesis there. He married (and later divorced and remarried), moved

---

[1]For an interesting reminiscence of Bly at Harvard, see Hall (1992).

back to Minnesota, first to Madison, then, years later, to Minneapolis, where he currently makes his home. He has traveled extensively — sometimes seemingly incessantly — especially during the past twenty or twenty-five years.

Bly's first book of poetry, *Silence in the Snowy Fields* (1962), immediately established him as a new and important lyric voice in contemporary American poetry. His work was widely admired and often imitated. His second book, *The Light Around the Body* (1967), which won the National Book Award, made conspicuously evident Bly's strong social and political views, especially his extremely outspoken castigation of the Vietnam War and, explicitly, his criticism of the American involvement in Vietnam. The dichotomy represented by these two early books has continued to define Bly's career. Likewise, both his lyrical voice and his controversial stands on social and political issues have continued throughout the years, though they are often curiously mixed together. Thus, Bly's work has been dealt with in widely divergent ways by his critics. Furthermore, Bly has himself actively contributed to the critical, personal, poetic, social, and political debate that has surrounded his work, and he has been extremely productive as a critic in his own right.

Bly has published a dozen major books of his own poetry, numerous collections of his translations of other poets (among them Georg Trakl, César Vallejo, Juan Ramón Jiménez, Pablo Neruda, Federico García Lorca, Gunnar Ekelöf, Tomas Tranströmer, Kabir, Olav H. Hauge, Rainer Maria Rilke, Antonio Machado, and many others) as well as scores of reviews and critical essays on poets, poetry, and his own poetic theories and practices.

In recent years Bly has been particularly active and visible (no contemporary poet is more immediately recognizable) as a spokesman for "women's" and "men's" groups and has spent a large portion of his time, both in this country and abroad, giving lectures and holding seminars on fairy tales, old stories and legends, and poems in terms of their relationships to modern life and in terms of men's and women's relationships with each other. These activities and Bly's theories on the men's movement came to culmination with his publication of *Iron John: A Book About Men* (1990) which immediately soared to the top of the best-seller charts, and which led to Bly's increasingly frenetic schedule of readings, and to his invitations to meetings, lectures, and seminars on a wide variety of social, political, and literary topics. At the same time, Bly continued to produce poems, translations, essays and reviews, and to give readings of his own poetry and of many other writers' work throughout the United States and worldwide.

Thus even though Bly has been active as poet, literary and social critic, translator, editor, and lecturer for more than forty years, his career seems to be far from over, his canon still incomplete. This survey of the criticism Bly's writing has occasioned will concentrate on his poetry — clearly his major work — and consider his career and the sizable body of that criticism chronologically.[2] It will include coverage of reviews and review-essays of his individual books of poetry as well as critical articles, sections of books devoted to him, and detailed, chapter by chapter coverage of each of the complete books published on Bly and his work to date. Each chapter will be organized to follow this sequence, in chronological order, and the first chapter, "The Poetry of the New Imagination," will include, in addition to a survey of the criticism of *Silence in the Snowy Fields*, detailed coverage of the beginning of and background to Bly's poetic career. This introductory chapter will also survey and summarize Bly's own approaches to literary criticism and examine the ways in which his theories of literature have influenced both his own poetry and the body of commentary his critics have devoted to his poetry. Other critical apparatuses (such as interviews and videocassette recordings) more pertinent to the later stages of Bly's career will be introduced at the relevant points in the survey of his career. Finally, an appendix on *Iron John: A Book About Men*, Bly's controversial best-seller on the "men's movement," will cover the critical and cultural attention that this important book has received — especially as it bears on Bly's poetry and his poetic career.

Since Bly has been an active and energetic critic and commentator on theory and poetic practice (his own and that of other poets') throughout his career, and because his criticism can hardly be separated from his poetry and other writings, this survey, in addition to covering the most significant work of the critics who have written on him, will include specific and detailed references to (and commentary on) Bly's own substantial critical commentary.

There are at present no definitive, detailed studies of the history of criticism on Robert Bly's work. This book, therefore, like the other volumes in the *Literary Criticism in Perspective* series, attempts to fill that void. The most substantial earlier survey of the criticism of Bly's work can be found in the introduction to *Critical Essays on Robert Bly*, edited by William V. Davis (New York: G. K. Hall, 1992). In addition, two bibliographies of primary and secondary materials are available: William H. Roberson's *Robert Bly: A Primary and Secondary Bibliography* (Metuchen, N. J.: Scarecrow Press, 1986), which is annotated and com-

---

[2]*What Have I Ever Lost by Dying?*, 1992, will be treated together with *The Morning Glory*, 1975, and *This Body Is Made of Camphor and Gopherwood*, 1977, since it contains many poems revised and reprinted from the earlier books. (See chapter four.)

prehensive, covering materials through 1984; and "A Bly Bibliography" in Victoria Frenkel Harris's *The Incorporative Consciousness of Robert Bly* (Carbondale: Southern Illinois University Press, 1992), which is selective and lists materials up to 1990.

The bibliography at the end of this book is divided into two separate sections listing the works cited in the text by Bly and by his critics. Both sections are arranged chronologically.

1: The Poetry of the New Imagination: *Silence in the Snowy Fields*

EVEN BEFORE ROBERT BLY HAD PUBLISHED his first book of poetry, *Silence in the Snowy Fields* (1962), the critical reaction to his work had begun. Citing several lines from Bly's "Driving Toward the Lac Que Parle River," Donald Hall, picking up the term *new imagination*, which Bly had used in his first published essay on poetry (1958), attempts to describe the "kind of imagination new to American poetry" that he finds in Bly's work and in the work of several of his contemporaries (1962, 24, 38). Bly's poetry, although it makes use of a colloquial vocabulary and a special diction, is, according to Hall, "subjective but not autobiographical" (25). And, although it initially seems to come from an "irrational" imagination, the "inward" images make for a "profound subjectivity" that, as Nelson argues, might finally be taken as a "description of intuition itself" (1984, 20, 24). If at least one critic (Brooks, 1963) contradicts these estimates of Bly's early work, most others find *Silence in the Snowy Fields* and Robert Lowell's *Life Studies* (1959) the two "most revolutionary and influential" books of the period and, as Saunders says, books that usher in a "revolution against intellectualism and impersonality" and create an ongoing movement toward "intuition and the experiential" (1978, 353).

Once *Silence in the Snowy Fields* was published, the critical reaction was immediate, surprisingly widespread for a first book, and primarily positive. There were almost forty reviews of it in this country and more than another half dozen when the book appeared in Great Britain five years later. Reviewers frequently describe the poems in terms of their simplicity, which is called impressive (Anonymous, 1962), deceptive (Anonymous, 1963/1964), earnest (Derleth, 1963), heavy (Anonymous, 1967), monotonous (Hughes, 1963), boring (Jerome, 1963), fresh (Stepanchev, 1963), and achieved (Nordell, 1963). Indeed, the word *simplicity* becomes a constant in Bly's critical canon over the years. Nelson begins his book on Bly positively by referring to the "pronounced simplicities" of the poems in *Silence in the Snowy Fields* (1984, 1); Rehder, on the other hand, calls Bly's simplicity his "effort to keep [his] special pleading under control" (1992, 281).

Reviewers of *Silence in the Snowy Fields* find the poems themselves intensely subjective (Stepanchev, 1963) or studiously "irrational"

(Clunk, 1962), but subtle (Colombo, 1963) and evocatively abstract (Hamilton, 1967) meditations that end in "silence, without complaint" (Fowlie, 1963), written in a "confirmed" but effective naiveté (Guest, 1965) that represents a spiritual journey (Wheat, 1967) and celebrates "a world without evil" (Gunn, 1963). Two reviews in particular set the tone and point the direction for the more substantial critical responses to follow. Louis Simpson calls *Silence in the Snowy Fields* "one of the few original and stimulating" books of poetry published "in recent years" and sees it as providing a solution to those "bored with the status quo," those who "hope for a new poetry" (1963, 139). Ralph J. Mills, Jr. recognizes in *Silence in the Snowy Fields* "a poetry of concentrated understatement," in which the imagery "bears the weight of the experience presented," resulting in poems that "move outward to interpret the world" with a "pointed moral sense" (1963, 341, 344).

The critical articles took up where the reviewers left off. In their attempt to place this new poet who had so abruptly appeared, critics took their first clues from Bly himself, and the major criticism of his early work, like that of his work to the present moment, has been the exploration of how poems like those in *Silence in the Snowy Fields* (and the later "snowy fields" poems in *This Tree Will Be Here for a Thousand Years*, 1979) had grown out of earlier poetic traditions (Chinese, European, and South American[1]) and, even more importantly, philosophical, mystical, and psychological traditions, especially those associated with the writings of C. G. Jung.

In an important sense, the criticism of Bly's early work took its lead and direction not only from the poetry itself but also from the premises put forward by the critics in an attempt to deal with this poetry of the new imagination. As Lensing and Moran (1976, 57-58) succinctly point out,

> In their preoccupation with the kind of poetry different from that being written by their contemporaries, the poets of the Emotive Imagination have also been concerned with the need for a different criticism, one which will provide a vocabulary and set of premises by which their own work can be justly evaluated. "New kinds of criticism will have to be developed in the coming years," Simpson [1967] explicitly asserts. It is Bly, however, who has been chiefly concerned with this need. . . .

---

[1]In an interview (1980, 250), Bly said that Antonio Machado, the important twentieth-century Spanish poet, was "the father" of *Silence in the Snowy Fields*. Cf. Molesworth (1979, 113): "One might well say, as Eliot said of Pound and Chinese poetry, that Bly has invented South American poetry for our time."

"We need a criticism which begins all over again — a criticism which attempts to distinguish what is poetry from what is not" [Bly, 1962a, 79].

Lensing and Moran prefer to use the term *emotive imagination* (rather than Hall's *new imagination* or any of the other definitions coined by critics) in their attempts to define these new poems being written by Bly and others. Other definitions of these poems, in which "the unconscious is speaking to the unconscious" as Rothenberg says, include the terms *deep image* (Rothenberg, 1963), *subjective-image* (Stepanchev, 1965), *image-poem* (Kelly, 1963), and *phenomenalism* (Locke, 1964). Lensing and Moran identify James Wright, Louis Simpson, and William Stafford in addition to Bly as central figures of this new movement in poetry in which, as Piccione characterizes it, the "poem emerges not as a statement *about* the mystical (or perceptual) experience, but as the process itself, the recreation and transmission of an essentially non-rational glimpse at cosmic vision" (1970, 31).

With his *manifesto-criticism* (Lensing and Moran, 1976, 59), most clearly evidenced in his magazine *The Fifties* (later called *The Sixties* and then *The Seventies)*, Bly took the lead in pointing a direction for this criticism that "begins all over again." He argued that poetry should be "responsive entirely to the imagination" and should awaken man's "bypassed emotions, ignored feelings, unexplained thoughts" — that it should "express thoughts not yet thought" (1962a, 66). Further, he believed that the good poets were already at work and that good poetry was already available to readers. "What we lack," he said, is "good criticism" (79) to accompany these poets and that poetry. Bly felt that the critical climate of the 1960s was irresponsible, that "about 1960 all responsible criticism stopped" (Bly, 1981-82).[2] And this climate, according to Bly, created an "odd situation" in which "more bad poetry" was being "published now than ever before in American history" — at the same time that "most of the reviews are positive" (Bly, 1978).

In an interview (Dodd, 1978), Bly described his own early work in criticism by saying that he wanted "precisely to attack" the earlier

[2]Bly was responding here to an article by Frederick Turner (1980), who acknowledged in reply that Bly had been "one of the 'point-men' of his generation" and that he had broken "uncomfortable intellectual ground," questioned the unquestionable, and cast a "cold eye upon the pieties, liberal or conservative, of the current fashion." Turner went on to state that Bly had reformulated his argument in a "more responsible, clearer, more tactful" and more applicable way than he himself had, and to call for "more poets . . . capable of the sheer logical lucidity and mental discipline Mr. Bly demonstrates."

"new criticism" of Allen Tate and Robert Penn Warren. "It was neces-
sary to clear some ground," he said. Furthermore, he argued, the
"normal process of human growth" involved "the new generation at-
tacking the older one. And attacking them strongly, wiping them out
as far as possible" (37). Bly made it clear that he meant this
"disappearance of criticism" hurt both poets and critics, that the
younger poets and critics "in failing to attack Merwin, or Rich, or Lev-
ertov, or me, or Ginsberg, or Simpson, or Hall, or Ed Dorn are not do-
ing their job" (38). Or, as he said elsewhere, "being rude to older po-
ets is just a way of clearing ground for yourself" (Bly, 1978).

Since Bly has taken such an active role as a critic over the years and
produced a sizeable body of criticism, it is surprising that his criticism
has never been systematically criticized (see Davis, 1992, 1) except in
the recent Ph.D. dissertation by Lammon (1991), which covers Bly's
critical commentary between 1958 and 1986. This study provides an
important addition to the larger canon of Bly's contributions to litera-
ture, both for what it shows about Bly's poetry and for the ways it
helps to map the field of literary criticism during this period and the
criticism of poetry in general.

Lammon argues that, although Bly is a part of the long tradition of
poets who have commented on poetry and poetics (William
Wordsworth, Samuel Taylor Coleridge, Ezra Pound, T. S. Eliot, and
Charles Olsen are mentioned specifically), his commentary differs
significantly from other and earlier "poet-critics" (10). Furthermore, he
says, Bly's critical methods deserve as much attention as his ideas do.
Focusing on Bly's essay "The Dead World and the Live World"
(1966a) as the best illustration of the process of Bly's critical commen-
tary, Lammon describes this process as a "'dialectic' of 'meditation'"
(116) whose terms involve a "provocation" (in which the reader is
"provoked . . . emotionally," both positively and negatively, and mo-
tivated by "a desire to heal"); this provocation is inevitably followed
by a "revocation," a "calling back" to the "original reasoning"
(through literary, social, and intellectual history) "implicit in [the] im-
ages"; and this revocation is then followed by an ongoing
"convocation," the "synthesis of ideas" that has been "generated from
the author's claims and the reader's response" (116-17).

Lammon (1991a) argues that Bly's critical commentary depends es-
sentially on his "unorthodox ideas about the imagination" and, there-
fore, that his critical discourse does not resemble traditional scholarly
literary criticism — which Bly himself often denounces. Lammon
identifies three phases in Bly's criticism. He defines these as the
"public, argumentative, instructive" "polemical" phase, the "more
private, impressionistic, intuitive" "meditative" phase, and the
"increasingly obscure, tangential, prophetic" "visionary" phase. (In

this tripartite division of Bly's critical career, Lammon, as he clearly acknowledges, is following the classification first put forward by Unterecker in his foreword to Nelson's 1984 study of Bly.)

Obviously influenced by and indebted to the principals of reader-response criticism, Lammon further argues that, in order to appreciate Bly's critical commentary, his reader (or his subsequent critic) "needs to be a conspirator rather than a disinterested observer," a "'dialectical reader' who is willing to participate in the imaginative leaps and unexplained references typical of Bly's prose," so that an "inter-textual dialectic" may be established between Bly — as both poet and critic — and his critics. (This has always been the approach that most of Bly's most sympathetic and perceptive critics have taken with respect to his work, although, as will be seen, the approach has not by any means been universally advocated or defended.)

Bly's critical position, as outlined by Lammon, is essentially opposed to the more traditional and more immediately and more definitively endorsed positions advocated by influential critics like Northrop Frye and others. Frye, "interested in some of the same topics Robert Bly takes up in his commentary" (Lammon, 1991, 13), challenges the "limitations" of a poet-critic like Bly. Indeed, Frye (1957) argues that it is hardly possible for a poet, taking on the role of a critic, "to avoid expanding his own tastes . . . intimately linked to his own practice, into a general law of literature." Furthermore, Frye argues, the poet, "speaking as critic," writes "not criticism, but documents to be examined by critics." In a 1971 study, Frye elaborates on his earlier argument to suggest that any critic who accepts a poet's critical commentary as a directive for his own criticism drastically compromises his own analysis of the work in question. Frye argues that criticism is a "theory of literature" and not just a "minor and non-essential element of its practice" (14) and that the poet's relationship to poetry is, therefore, identical to the critic's relationship to criticism but that these two roles should not (or cannot) overlap. This is a position that Bly (as well as many of his critics) strongly disagrees with.[3] Lammon, quite rightly, points out that the "scholar is just as liable to the pressures of prejudice" (15) as the poet might be, but, be that as it may, and in spite of differences between Bly's own work as critic and the work of more

---

[3]See, for instance, Bly 1959, 1959a, 1959b, 1962c, 1963, 1966a, 1966b, and 1966c. Although it would no doubt *not* be the case that Bly would argue against what Frye (1971) described as the "final steps" in his argument — namely, that criticism must "develop a sense of history within literature" to "complement the historical criticism that relates literature to its non-literary historical background"; that it must develop "its own form of historical overview" based on "what is inside literature rather than [what is] outside it" (24)

"scholarly" critics like Frye, Bly's "brand of criticism is both invigorating and useful" (18), and it leaves one "changed forever" (25).

Throughout his career the most direct criticism of Bly's literary criticism has come by way of indirection, as ad hominem attacks on Bly himself or on Bly as editor or anthologist. Several classic early instances of such attacks can be found in Jones (1963) and Sorrentino (1963), both of whom attack Bly as editor of his magazine *The Sixties*. Jones calls Bly and William Duffy, his co-editor, "ignorant fools" and says that *The Sixties* represents the "easy ineptitude of Mr. Bly's critical judgment." Sorrentino, in what purports to be a review of Bly's, Duffy's, and James Wright's *The Lion's Tail and Eyes: Poems Written Out of Laziness and Silence* (1962), refers to "Mr. Bly and Co." as "stupid" and "cornshuckers."

These kinds of attacks, however, were countered by others, including reminiscences of the "first faint shock of new energy" (Haines, 1981) generated by *The Fifties* and *The Sixties*, and by historical recapitulations of the period and of the way that Bly's magazine helped to "break up the stifling insularity that had smothered American poetry for so long" — especially in the "narrow and constricted time" of the 1950s and the 1960s (Rutsala, 1989). Zavatsky (1981) takes Bly at his word in his call for criticism of his work, and his essay offers interesting and helpful comments on a number of important elements that occur and recur throughout the course of Bly's career.

The most definitive critical comments on *The Fifties* and *The Sixties* (and on Bly's Sixties Press) are to be found in Zweig's 1966 essay evaluating Bly's critical contributions both in his magazine and through his press. Zweig argues that Bly's "dangerous enterprise," his "erratic, single-handed experiment," involves the "desire to test the limits" of American poetic traditions, to "weed out" the "dry exercises" of the past and, following poets like Walt Whitman, Hart Crane, and Theodore Roethke, to attempt to "follow [his] imagination into whatever hard country it would lead."[4]

Furthermore, and well worth noting, it is also the case, as Hall has shown, that Bly has always given a "cordial response to negative criticism" as long as there is "an *idea* lurking in the denunciation" (1981, 35). Indeed, as Bly himself said, "Criticism does not imply contempt. The criticism of my own poetry that has been [of] the most use to me

---

[4]For a summary of the work of the Sixties Press and the various responses to it see Hamilton (1973); cf. Lammon (1991, 80-82, 137-38). For a consideration of Bly in terms of the Whitman-Crane-Roethke tradition see Williams (1977). See also Bly's essay "Whitman's Line as a Public Form"(1986c) in his *Selected Poems*.

has been criticism that, when I first heard it, utterly dismayed me" (1967c; cf. Jones and Daniels, 1981, v).

Molesworth likewise (1975, 1979) addresses Bly's role as critic in the early essays Bly contributed to his journal *The Fifties* and *The Sixties* and suggests a relationship between that early criticism and the poetry Bly was writing at that time. Molesworth finds Bly's early criticism (like the journals themselves) "feisty, but never querulous" and Bly's "negative strictures" always "energetically expressed." He feels that the "poetry needed the theorizing" to "clear space" for itself; in short, as he says, "one is most struck by Bly's balanced criticism," particularly during a time when "few other critics" were able to assess the work of contemporary poets "with any sort of balance" (1979, 115, 188).

In *News of the Universe: Poems of Twofold Consciousness* (1980) Bly traces the history of poetry through a selection of about 150 poems from the eighteenth century to the present. He arranges these poems in chronological categories that he calls "The Old Position," "The Attack on the Old Position," "Poems of Twofold Consciousness" (grouped into two phases, the early twentieth century, and from 1945 to 1979), "The Object Poem," and "Leaving the House." He introduces each of these sections with a short essay on the period in question and concludes the book with meditative essays on Goethe (1980c) and Yeats (1980d). This unique anthology constitutes Bly's criticism of the history of poetry during the past several centuries. As such, it is an important book for both Bly and his critics, even though, surprisingly enough, it has largely been overlooked by most of them. Davis (1982a, 1988) is one exception.

By quoting Jacob Boehme ("We are all asleep in the outward man") in his epigraph to *Silence in the Snowy Fields*, Bly suggested one source for his work that has been exhaustively explored, if not yet fully mined, by his critics. Howard (1969), Gitzen (1976), and Davis (1979-80) discuss in detail various aspects of the Boehmean influences on Bly's early work. Howard focuses on the inward-outward dichotomy in Bly's poetry. He argues that the "real burden" of this poetry "coincides with Bly's real body" (43) and that this burden is, literally, that "of a body transfigured by the weight of its own death" (38) — a clear allusion to the title poem of Bly's second book, *The Light Around the Body* (1967). Gitzen concentrates on Bly's use of imagery and the parallel associations between Bly's and Boehme's use of similar images (especially the relationship between light and spirit). Davis develops the relationship between Bly and Boehme in even greater detail, considering Bly's concept of the "two worlds" as well as the light-dark dichotomy and extending his argument to treat the development of a private and public language in Bly's early work (including the public language of both *Silence in the Snowy Fields* and *The Light Around the Body*) as an outgrowth of Bly's interest in Boehme and Boehme's influence on this early poetry.

Another important component in Bly's somewhat unsystematic system of criticism has to do with his notion of "leaps," or what he calls "leaping poetry." As Molesworth indicates, the leap becomes for Bly "a way back to a different order of understanding" since "the missing truth" has left its "traces, its broken and frayed connections" that can be "spark[ed] into conductivity" in the poem (1978b, 326). This notion of leaping poetry, Molesworth argues, is one of the natural outgrowths of Bly's essential theory of literature that is so much at odds with the "conspiracy of rationality and order" evidenced by the academic critics (325).

Bly's most incisive comments on his notions of leaping poetry (and leaps occur in his poetry throughout his career) can be found in several essays (Bly, 1967d, 1972b) as well as in his *Leaping Poetry: An Idea with Poems and Translations* (1975), which one reviewer calls "a fabulous, madly lucid, useful little book" (Anonymous, 1975b) and in his anthology of "tiny" poems, *The Sea and the Honeycomb* (1966), which has been called "an extremely useful book" (Anonymous, 1967a) and "one of the most valuable of recent books" (Clayre, 1967). (Cf. Nelson [1984, 113-27].)

The Boehmean trappings in Bly were quickly associated with the term *deep image*, still not adequately defined by the critical community even though much of the most important criticism of Bly's early work is associated with various theories of deep image poetics. Melnyczuk (1988) defines deep image poetry as a technique in which the poet juxtaposes "radically disparate images aimed at detonating an emotional explosion in the reader." When Myers and Simms (1985) attempt to define the term, which they associate with the older and more clearly defined *anagoge*, they quote Bly's essay on Francis Ponge (1980a) in which he links the image to the psyche and the unconscious. Bly has regularly suggested that "the unconscious passes into the object and returns" during the writing of deep image poems (1980a, 107). For him, the anagogical associations are most clearly aligned with Rilke, a poet he has translated and clearly learned from. For an analysis of Bly's relationship to deep image poetry and its traditions, see Breslin (1984, 176-81).

Altieri (1979) and Haskell (1979) describe in greatest detail the rather elaborate critical framework that has grown up around deep image poetics. In an essay in which Roberson quite rightly detects "an underlying sense of acrimony" (1986, 165), Altieri places Bly within the "self-consciously postmodern" traditions of *radical presence* that surfaced in the 1960s as the direct result of dissatisfaction with the "epistemological and cultural implications of the New Critical aesthetic" and created the "varieties of immanentist experience" practiced by Bly and others (78). According to Altieri, Bly is able to use the theory and practice of deep image poetics to adapt "his theological model" in "thoroughly secular terms" and thereby "leave the reader with a new level of awareness" (85-86). In a substantial, wide-ranging article in which he calls the deep image movement "a mode of seeing" or vision as much as a poetic technique, Haskell describes Bly as "the most active spokesman for the deep image movement" (140-41). Even though Haskell feels that, along with confessional verse, deep image poetry is one of the two most important strands in American poetry since World War II, he acknowledges that the final value of deep image poetry is difficult to judge .

The issue of deep image poetry and Bly's specific use of it in his early poems engaged the attention of a number of critics, who, not surprisingly, came to rather diverse conclusions with respect to Bly's use of deep images and to the success or failure of his early work in general.

Mills finds in the poems of Bly and James Wright, Bly's close friend, fellow poet, coeditor (*The Lion's Tail and Eyes: Poems Written Out of Laziness and Silence*, 1962), and, with Bly, cotranslator of Georg Trakl (*Twenty Poems of Georg Trakl*, 1961), an "intense subjectivity" and moments of "extreme perception" that derive from "subliminal regions of the mind" and are "joined by associations of an emotional, symbolic, and lyrical kind" and thus are "capable of stirring subtle and profound responses in the reader" (1965, 212). Friberg calls Bly's deep image poems "reminiscent of Emerson's notions of "poetic creativity" (1977, 208-9). Molesworth sees both positive and negative possibilities in Bly's use of deep images. On the one hand, he finds positive and effective Bly's disciplined concentration on images that "lead through the self, beyond the self" to create a "curious mix" of "pastoral quietism and moral harangue"; on the other, he points out that there are clear risks involved in such deep image poetry, which, he argues, might easily result in an "endless series of sensory fragments" (1979, 145). Kramer argues that Bly's successful poetry always depends on a "poetic rather than on an esoteric context" and that his genuine achievement as a poet "has little to do with deep images" (1983, 449). Kalaidjian, in one of the few negative estimates of Bly's use of deep images in his early poetry, argues that the "essential conservative aesthetic" of deep imagery has drained the poems in *Silence in the Snowy Fields* of their "discursive power" and thus diminishes them (1989, 127).

In another important recent and largely negative essay, Rehder addresses the form of "virtually all" of Bly's poems and notes that typically in a Bly poem experience is seen from the "inside" in such a way that there is an "explicit or implied world of consciousness and unconsciousness — and the merging" of the two. This creates a "double pressure" in Bly's work: the attempt to accommodate the unconscious and at the same time to "resist meeting the idea and its consequences head-on." Thus, Bly writes poems in which "the action is thinking" and that are, therefore, "fragments of an autobiography that seeks to hide its true nature." In this sense Bly's successions of images are a "substitute for analysis" and his metaphors, in their "incongruity," are a "sign of confusion" because "their inner connection is unclear" (1992, 270, 274, 277). Furthermore, Rehder believes that the term "deep image," as it has been applied to Bly's poems, is a "misnomer" because the "depth has been ironed out" of too many of the poems (especially some of the most celebrated ones, like "Driving Toward the Lac Que Parle River"). Whereas other critics refer to Bly's use of deep images in terms of the "minimalism" of understatement, Rehder calls it "a refusal to engage in self-analysis" and comes to the conclusion that "there is no 'deep image' in any of these poems." Likewise, Rehder finds Bly's appropriation of Boehme and Jung a refusal to confront the unconscious and a "denial of reality" (275, 280, 281).

Nevertheless, although Kalaidjian's and Rehder's comments are much more recent than most of the criticism already cited, they do not represent any reversal of the majority position — that Bly's theory and practice of deep image poetics has been not only a pervasive but also a positive force in American poetry, and that it has been used successfully in many of his most memorable poems, early and late, as well as in many of the most celebrated poems of his contemporaries.

Finally, as Smith and Taylor say, Bly's use of deep images makes it possible for readers and critics to "journey inward" themselves, as the poems do. Indeed, Bly's images tend to "'drop' the reader into mythic reality" and force him to come to some sort of understanding of himself in terms of the "two worlds" of his consciousness (Smith and Taylor, 1986, 113; cf. Bly, 1972).Therefore, as Dodd says, after *Silence in the Snowy Fields*, readers will never be "quite the same again" (1992, 113).

Nelson, in the first major comprehensive study of Bly's work published in this country (it was preceded by Friberg's, published in Sweden in 1977), describes *Silence in the Snowy Fields* as a "rebellious" book in which Bly flies in the face of "narrow and atrophied poetic standards" (1984, 2–3). As such, *Silence in the Snowy Fields* signals the end of one era and the beginning of another. Primarily engaged in the explication and analysis of individual poems and heavily dependent on Bly's theories and interviews to support his readings of the book, both as a whole and in its individual poems, Nelson focuses on Bly's poetic sources, his use of deep images, his overt use of Jungian trappings, and the way in which the repetition of key images unifies and enriches the book. He concludes that *Silence in the Snowy Fields* "should be read as if it were a single poem" and that its final impact is "greater than the sum of its parts" (8, 29).

In the preface to his book Sugg (1986) stresses the universality of Bly's "spiritual themes" and his "pervasive commitment" to imagery and themes "best described by Jungian psychology." Following Bly's "inward journey through the psyche" throughout his career, and seeing Bly's career as "a synecdoche for the development of American poetry from the early fifties to the present," Sugg identifies, in his chapter on *Silence in the Snowy Fields*, Bly's two major themes as "an elucidation of human nature as twofold" and the exploration of the relationship between man's "twofold consciousness and Nature" (3, 5, 21). These themes work in such a way, Sugg argues, that the "emergent inner man" is revealed. He "gently" criticizes Bly's tone in *Silence in the Snowy Fields* at the same time that he acknowledges that Bly's poetry "has always been an acquired taste" (22, 23).

Adapting her "interpretative methods as much as possible to Bly's aesthetic" and guiding her study of the "incorporative consciousness" of the lyric side of Bly's career (she gives short shrift to Bly's "political" poems) by the defining limits of attempting "to become the kind of reader Bly's work implies that it requires," Harris (1992, 8, 9) presents a reading of *Silence in the Snowy Fields* that stresses the "dialogic" nature of Bly's work and the "strong intellectual backdrop" behind it at the same time that it illuminates the individual poems she selects for analysis (29-30). Harris finds in Bly's work "an early feminist critique of culture" (34). This perspective, given the advantages of hindsight, anticipates in Bly's early work an issue that was to become much more overt — and much more controversial — later on in his career, especially in *The Man in the Black Coat Turns* (1981) and *Loving a Woman in Two Worlds* (1985), and even more definitively in his extra poetic activities related to the organization of men's groups throughout the country, the debates stirred up by these activities, and his best selling nonfiction book *Iron John: A Book About Men* (1990).[5] Harris's thesis, however, is argued toward her own ends, and the poems she chooses for analysis often seem to have been chosen because they are (at least in her view) weighted in the direction of that thesis.

Davis argues that *Silence in the Snowy Fields* is Bly's most important book, "a paradigm for the journey which Bly's work *in toto* takes"; it is, he says, the single book that "establishes the bases" of all of Bly's

[5]See the Appendix, "*Iron John: A Book About Men* and the Critics."

work and, therefore, permits the reader "to read the rest of his work intelligently" (1988, 17). Davis describes the long apprenticeship that leads up to *Silence in the Snowy Fields*; discusses the structure, the organization, and the dominate themes and metaphors Bly uses in the book; and analyzes a number of the most important poems from the book in an attempt to provide readers with an understanding of Bly's early career. For a basic analysis of the backgrounds to *Silence in the Snowy Fields*, as well as for specific details on the organization, structure, and development of the individual sections of the book and an interpretation of key poems within it, this is probably the best book with which to begin a critical study of Bly's work.

Bly's own critical writings during this period — simultaneous with the writing of his early poems — provide, as has already been suggested, important buttressing both to the poems themselves and to the criticism of the poems. Indeed, it can be argued that Bly's critical comments constitute an important and necessary complement to (if they are not literally part of) the history of the literary criticism of his work during this early portion of this career — as, indeed, they do in every stage of his career. This is the case for several reasons: first, Bly has been a prolific critic and commentator on poetry throughout his career; second, even when he is not commenting specifically on his own poetic practice, his comments are relevant to that practice (sometimes in ways that are surprising); third, most of Bly's best critics have made use of his essays, reviews, and incidental comments as bases or supplemental illuminations for their own comments and critical theories, as well as for their critical analyses of his poetry; finally, as Bly's poetry has gone through various stages (and through frequent revisions), so too have his theoretical bases shifted to keep pace with his poetic practices, a circumstance that makes inevitable the relationship between the poems and the theories, and vice versa. Therefore, a brief summary of the most significant of Bly's remarks on matters relevant to these early poems is not only pertinent to any history of the literary criticism of his work but necessary to a full understanding of the analysis of the criticism itself.

William Matthews says that "poets who are also critics always," when writing about poems by other poets, also write, "in an elaborate code," about their own poems — "both those they have written and those they aspire to write." Since Matthews, himself a poet, is without a doubt right, and since Bly has been such a prolific and controversial poet and critic, one who has "annoyed many and threatened not a few," Bly's criticism constitutes a necessary, inevitable, and invaluable commentary on his poetry. It is simply one more way in which Bly is unique among his contemporaries. Indeed, as Matthews says, "It is nearly impossible to over-emphasize the importance of Bly's criticism" (1969, 49). Gregory Orr, another poet, says that poets must write the essays on poetry "that only poets can write," and then he argues that Bly's essays, in the historical context of the mid-1950s, are the "most intense public thinking" about the "human importance" of poetry that is "taking place in English" during this period (1981, 116, 120).

Not all critics or literary historians would agree that Bly's prose pieces and interviews constitute an inevitable or even useful association with his poetry, and some of them would apparently argue that theory and practice exist at a considerable remove from one another — at least in Bly's case. Perkins, for instance, says, "My objection, I should make clear, is both to Bly's ideas and especially to his expression of them" (1987, 568). It is perhaps important to note that Perkins may well be responding more to Bly's followers (both poets and critics), who have often carried his ideas to extremes (both in their criticism and in their poetry). Just before his comment on Bly, Perkins quotes Orr, who argues that the art of poetry demands "intense, naïve enthusiasm," and "an unexamined intellectual and emotional energy" that is "opposed to logical analysis and critical thinking" (118)!

Bly's essays (he has published more than two hundred to date) and reviews began to appear in the late 1950s, several years before *Silence in the Snowy Fields* was published in 1962. Shortly after *Silence in the Snowy Fields* appeared, Bly consented to his first interview. There have been more than fifty since then. Some of these pieces are brief, and (as Lammon, 1991, and others have shown) Bly has never attempted in them to engage in any consistent, coherent, critical analysis or to create any specific analytical system. There are numerous contradictions and inconsistencies in his comments and criticism over the years. Nonetheless, as a body they constitute an elaborate critical apparatus that exists alongside of and is interwoven with Bly's poetry, an apparatus that cannot be, and has not been, ignored by his readers and his critics — even though, as has already been pointed out, it has more frequently been referred to than criticized.[6]

[6]If Bly's criticism, important as it is to a full understanding and analysis of his total career, has not received much in the way of critical commentary, his substantial body of work as a translator has received even less attention, although, as Howard Nelson remarks, it is quite possible that Bly's translations "have had an even greater influence on contemporary American poetry than his original work" (1984, 37). Thus, though these two chapters of Bly's career still remain to be written (and criticized), surely it would be the case, as Davis says, that Bly's work as critic and translator would be in a very real sense "inseparable from his poetry" in any final analysis of his full career (1992, 1). For representative comments on Bly's role as a translator see on the positive side Stitt (1963), Benedikt (1968), Carroll (1979), Rolf (1981),

In several essays published in the early 1960s Bly summarizes in a kind of critical commentary his thinking during the time he was writing the poems in *Silence in the Snowy Fields*. In contrast to the nineteenth century, he notes, with its habitual "feeling of constriction," the present involves a "mood of infinite expansion" and there are now signs that "poetry is beginning again" in this time (Bly, 1961, 350, 354). French poetry voyages into the imagination, unlike American poetry, which fears the unconscious (Bly, 1961a, 66, 68); American poets therefore need to trust the unconscious and cultivate their solitude. In a major statement entitled "A Wrong Turning in American Poetry" Bly (1963, reprinted 1990) says that since 1917 twentieth-century American poetry has moved through three clearly distinguished "psychic" stages, each associated with one generation. He calls these the "objective," the "metaphysical," and the "hysterical" generations. According to Bly, all of this poetry is "outward" poetry, without any "spiritual development" and thus unlike the poetry written by "the great poets of this century" — poets like Neruda, Vallejo, Jiménez, Machado, and Rilke, who had written from their own "inwardness" poems that penetrate "into the unconscious" (1963, 35, 38, 47). Elsewhere, Bly (1960) argues that poets writing in the "new style" and with the "new imagination" must write like the great poets of the past.

The critical positions on Bly at the end of this first stage of his career are most succinctly summarized by Dodd and Heyen. Dodd says that in *Silence in the Snowy Fields* Bly discovered the "spirit" of the American landscape "breathing in and through" the words of his poems and that, having experienced *Silence in the Snowy Fields*, the "body of America was never again the same to us," never merely "external"; that Bly's description of the "knowledge of our geographical lives" in these poems has become a "given" that, "once gained," one can "never go back from: like self-consciousness" (1993, 107). Heyen, ad-

---

and Hass (1982); and on the negative side Anonymous (1974a), Eshleman (1964, 1971/1972), Agee (1981), and Heller (1982). Something of the controversy that surrounded this debate can be seen in several of the critical comments. Lehman (1985), responding to Bly's translations of Rilke as reported on by Hass (1982), and quoting Hass — who had contended that one of Rilke's early poems was less interesting than Bly's "vigorous, unrhymed, unmetered translation" of it — asks, "Imagine if you can the same method applied to *Paradise Lost*." And in one early estimate that has sparked additional commentary both by Bly and his critics, Gullans (1970) says that Bly and his various collaborators on translations have "long been enthusiastic about poems written in languages they do not understand." See Bly's *The Eight Stages of Translation* (1983) for his own most definitive statement of his theories of translation.

mitting to his early dislike of the surprising and unexpected poems in *Silence in the Snowy Fields*, overcomes his "niggling" reservations when he discovers that "Bly's poems do not wear thin" and are "themselves suspensions of the critical faculty" (1969, 43).

These were simply other ways of saying that, in order to read Bly's poems of the "new imagination," critics needed to develop new imaginations themselves.

2: The Poetry of Protest:
The Light Around the Body
and "The Teeth Mother Naked at Last"

SEVERAL MONTHS BEFORE BLY PUBLISHED *The Light Around the Body* (1967), his most controversial book of poetry to date, he alerted his critics and readers to what might be expected in the new book and, at the same time, suggested several ways of approaching the kind of overt political poetry *The Light Around the Body* would contain. In separate versions of an essay published in England and America almost simultaneously, Bly (1967a, 1967b) said that "a poem can be a political act." He argued that the reason there had been "so few real political poems" published in America was that American poets fell into one of two groups: those who are "occasionally brave" in their public statements even though their poems have "not the slightest political energy"; and those who "fill their poems with political language" and then themselves "act like clowns," so that everyone will understand that they "don't really mean it." Bly lamented the fact that America had never produced a poet who "wrote great poetry," or "took a clear stand," and whose work itself had "serious political meaning." Clearly Bly saw himself as filling this void in American literature and life and was giving his critics advance notice of this fact.

The Light Around the Body filled the void; indeed, it created a poetic explosion not unlike the political explosion that the Vietnam War had created. This powerfully outspoken new book, so different both thematically and stylistically from *Silence in the Snowy Fields*, not only surprised — even shocked — Bly's critics and readers but forced them to reconsider their preconceived notions of what poetry ought to be and what Bly's poetry, judging from *Silence in the Snowy Fields*, conspicuously was. It also provided a thematic shock (new to American poetry, if not to the poetry Bly had been reading and obviously had been influenced by) by its overt political theses. Furthermore, Bly buttressed his politically outspoken poems with his energetic political activity as he traveled around the country reading and speaking out against the war in Vietnam and organizing rallies, demonstrations, and marches.

Although Bly's prose statements mentioned above had little specific impact on the immediate critical response to his new book, the blatantly outspoken political poems published in *The Light Around the Body* did. The book appeared during the height of the controversy over American involvement in Vietnam, and in it Bly named names (in "Asian Peace Offers Rejected without Publication," for instance, he wrote, "Men like Rusk are not men . . .").[1]

The critical reaction to *The Light Around the Body* began before the book was even published, when Wesleyan University Press, which had published *Silence in the Snowy Fields*, refused to publish *The Light Around the Body*, obviously afraid of the repercussions it would have. The critical fire was further fueled when *The Light Around the Body* won the National Book Award and Bly seized the opportunity of this public forum to speak out against the Vietnam War in person and to publicly challenge the young men in attendance at the NBA ceremony to resist the draft by turning over his award money to one of them and telling him, "I ask you to use this money . . . to counsel other young men . . . not to destroy their spiritual lives by participating in this war" (Bly, 1968, 14-15).

It was not surprising, then, that the reviews of *The Light Around the Body* focus heavily on the overt political poems in the central sections of the book, specifically entitled "The Vietnam War." The more than thirty reviews of *The Light Around the Body* (almost one fourth of them in British periodicals) suggest the wide variety of conflicting critical responses the book received. One American reviewer finds the book "weak poetically" and at the same time "dangerously alluring" and calls attention to the "curious externality" at work in Bly's words (Goldman, 1968). Other American critics call *The Light Around the Body* "an honorable failure" (Leibowitz, 1968), "monotonous in the cumulative effect" with political poems that are "predictable, even pious" (Mazzocco, 1968); a combination of conviction and "puckish nuttiness" (Burns, 1968); "arrogant and facile" (Carruth, 1968); filled with "weird oversimplifications" (Smith, 1968); even sentimental, shrilly melodramatic, posturing — in short (like *Silence in the Snowy Fields*), "another kind of arrogance" (Taylor, 1968).

More positively, other reviewers find in *The Light Around the Body* "a sadness for America" and see the book quietly translating and transforming the "inward mystery" that (thanks to Bly's indebtedness to the work of Jacob Boehme) had been the dominant voice in *Silence in the Snowy Fields* into "an expansive public language" (Zweig, 1968)

---

[1]In his *Selected Poems* (1986) Bly softened this line slightly to read, "Men like Rusk are not men only — . . . ". By then, a decade after *The Light Around the Body* had been published, he had conceded that "the exaggeration on both sides damaged the language of public debate" throughout the United States, even though he still believed that the "judging" had been "useful."

in *The Light Around the Body* — although four of the five sections of the book (the exception is the central section focused specifically on "The Vietnam War") are prefaced by epigraphs from Boehme and seem to suggest that, for Bly, these "two worlds" and these "two languages" are really only one world and one language.[2]

Such early estimates of *The Light Around the Body* culminate in several reviews that attempt to place the book in its own historical moment, both in its poetry and in the political protest it makes, and at the same time attempt to look through it, as it were, toward Bly's future. Zinnes, for instance, calls the book "one of the most significant American volumes to be published in years" (1968, 176). Simpson, noting Bly's debt to surrealism and to European and Spanish poets and mentioning his "arranging intelligence," his "original talent" and his "rare integrity," suggests that Bly is "one of the few poets in America from whom greatness can be expected" (1968, 74-75).

The British version of *The Light Around the Body* (1968) is quite different from the American one. It has fewer poems, the sequence of the poems is considerably changed, and the book is divided into three sections, not five. These factors somewhat change the thematic impact of the book (which would have been different in any case since the war in Vietnam was conspicuously an American war) and, at least in part, may well have influenced the somewhat different critical responses *The Light Around the Body* got in England and in America. Sugg makes the point that Bly's rearrangement of the poems in the British edition served to "tone down" the "sociopolitical thrust" of the American edition and to emphasize the theme of the "psychological development of consciousness" as the "key to social progress" as Bly seemed to posit "the perfection of the outer world upon the improvement of the inner world" (1986, 43).

The British reviewers tend to view the book either as a specifically American (and thus rather peripheral) product or in more general, and thus more international, terms. These reviewers argue that Bly's "darkness" and "inwardness" (which he had used effectively — as earlier critics and reviewers had noted — in *Silence in the Snowy Fields*) are much more deeply and fully felt and more effectively achieved here. This, some of these reviewers believe, largely has to do with

[2]The epigraph to the first section of *The Light Around the Body*, entitled "The Two Worlds," is from Boehme and clearly suggests Bly's theme for the book — a theme that many of his critics, early and late, failed to notice. The Boehmean passage reads, "For according to the outward man, we are in this world, and according to the inward man, we are in the inward world. . . . Since then we are generated out of both worlds, we speak in two languages, and we must be understood also by two languages" (Bly, 1967, 1; Bly's ellipsis).

Bly's being an American. Bland (1968), for instance, suggests that the "overly fey and self-indulgent" darkness of *Silence in the Snowy Fields* has been made "real" in *The Light Around the Body* and that Bly has here finally achieved the inwardness that was suggested, indeed promised, by *Silence in the Snowy Fields*. Other reviewers speak of *The Light Around the Body* in terms of its "generalized despair," which "gets lost in a haze of vague, over-reaching fantasy" or arbitrary details, so that the final political point of the book becomes either perfunctory or obvious (Brownjohn, 1968); or they document Bly's familiar mannerisms (Hamilton, 1968) and his political outrage as being more "forced than frightening" (Anonymous, 1968) and see him finally, if curiously, as the "currently fashionable American White Hope" (Symons, 1968).

Perhaps the most persistent of all the reviewers in attempting to see *The Light Around the Body* in an international context was Bly's long-time friend and admirer Kenneth Rexroth, who sees *The Light Around the Body* as the culmination of Bly's "struggle," both as poet and as critic (in the pages of his magazines *The Fifties* and *The Sixties*), "to return American poetry to the mainstream of international literature." The results of that struggle, Rexroth argues, make Bly one of the few poets who are "responsible" members of the international community and place him at the head of a poetic revival that has "returned American literature to the world community." Rexroth also briefly mentions *A Poetry Reading Against the Vietnam War*, the 1966 anthology by Bly and David Ray that was inspired by the antiwar readings Bly, Ray, and others had been giving on college campuses and was thus a kind of companion to *The Light Around the Body*. According to Rexroth, the anthology, like *The Light Around the Body*, was motivated by a responsibility for the survival of the human race (1967/68, 117-18).

There are few other reviews of *A Poetry Reading Against the Vietnam War*, and they focus primarily on the "propagandistic" content of the collection and on Bly's introduction to it, which is variously seen as "accusatory" (Lindenau, 1966) or as one of the finest pieces of writing on the Vietnam war (M. R., 1967). Nelson calls *A Poetry Reading Against the Vietnam War* a "devastating and eloquent collection" of materials (1984, 37), while Davis (1988, 73), quoting from Bly's preface that the "really serious evil of the war, rarely discussed, is the harm it will do the Americans inwardly" (Bly, 1966, 7), suggests that Bly has here anticipated his single most blatant antiwar poem, "The Teeth Mother Naked at Last" (1970).

The poetry of *The Light Around the Body* is protest poetry more than political poetry. This distinction is an important one, even though not all of Bly's critics make it. Mersmann, for instance, says that political poetry is "always in danger of being taken literally as prose" and that, read "as prose, the poems seem more strident and fantastic than they really are" (1974, 124). Davis argues that Bly's protest poetry is "cause oriented" and that Bly's causes are not always "overtly political ones." He concludes that "even [Bly's] most blatant political poems made more powerful poetic statements than they did political ones" and also points out that "not all of [Bly's] critics, then or now, agreed either with what he said or with the way in which he said it" (1992, 8).

Some critics, on the other hand, fail to notice the difference between the political and the protest poetry and, perhaps understandably, tend to confuse Bly's political actions and his protests as an individual citizen with his poetry of protest. If some of his critics open themselves to attacks because of this confusion, Bly, as they might well argue, and in some instances do argue, is himself frequently confusing — or simply confused. Certainly it could be argued that Bly, in his actions, his activism, and his words, often seems to be sending out confusing messages.

Most of Bly's critics, however, would agree, finally, that in *The Light Around the Body* and "The Teeth Mother Naked at Last" Bly had "reached a stage far in advance" of most other antiwar poets — so much so that what he had written in these poems went beyond protest poetry into what Gitlin (1971) calls political analysis.[3]

The poems in *The Light Around the Body* and "The Teeth Mother Naked at Last" are clearly Bly's most overt examples of the poetry of protest, and the critical response to these two works will be considered together here — for the sake of convenience if not exact chronology — because they are frequently dealt with in the same critical breath.[4] Nevertheless, it needs to be said that there remain clear differences among Bly's critics in their final estimates of these poems of protest and in their understanding of the poems' relevance to and impact on America and the Vietnam War specifically and their relevance to the general political situation worldwide.

Altieri argues that Robert Duncan is the only contemporary poet who has been successful in incorporating "the sufferings of the war in

[3]"The Teeth Mother Naked at Last" exists in three versions: the 1970 City Lights Books version (Bly, 1973d), the 1973 *Sleepers Joining Hands* version; and the revision of the *Sleepers Joining Hands* version published in Bly's *Selected Poems* (1986). The fullest critical treatments of the poem, focused on the final *Selected Poems* version, are the Davis analyses (1988, 73-78, and 1992a, 2126-29).

[4] Some critics, it should be noted, do insist on treating *The Light Around the Body* and "The Teeth Mother Naked at Last" quite separately. See, for instance, Lacey (1972).

Vietnam within his myth" (1979, 168). Cary Nelson expresses the view of several other critics in countering that this "claim seems difficult to sustain in the light of Bly's 'The Teeth Mother Naked at Last'" (1981, 143). Kalaidjian, also arguing for many other critics, contends that "The Teeth Mother Naked at Last" is a controversial work whose "high moral tone verges on the very propaganda it indicts" (1989, 133). Still other critics find in Bly's protest poetry a "voice choking on its own anger and going shrill" (Williamson, 1974) or a "political struggle" reduced to simple psychic melodrama" (Breslin, 1978) in which "the violence is Bly's own" (Hall, 1973). These charges are challenged by Heyen who, admitting to an initial suspicion with respect to Bly's work, had come to believe that Bly had found, in *The Light Around the Body*, a medium to bear the "weight of political protest poetically" so effectively that not a poem in the book is open to the charge that it is "essentially journalistic or propagandistic" pleading (1969, 49).

In his important study of Vietnam War poetry referred to earlier, Mersmann calls Bly "one of the most annoying and most exciting poets" of the period and attempts to place Bly's poetry within the context of Vietnam War poetry specifically and the larger context of modern war poetry in general. Noting that Bly seems "always to have sung soft songs to death," Mersmann speaks of Bly's "magnificent images of defeat" in *The Light Around the Body* and points out that the "tornadic emotions of Vietnam" convinced Bly that "the inward man could not survive unless the outward man spoke out" (1974, 113, 118-120). Several other critics also attempt to place Bly's protest poetry in the larger arena of theoretical discussion since, as Cary Nelson avers, American poetry "continually addresses the world at large" and "prophesies possibilities" (1981, 23).

Howard Nelson describes Bly as a poet who "takes on ambitious political and historical themes passionately" (1984, 39). Thus *The Light Around the Body* can be seen as Bly's attempt to "forge a language" (39) that can contain both the inward and outward worlds he had found in Boehme, explored in *Silence in the Snowy Fields* and in *The Light Around the Body*, and documented in his essay "Leaping Up into Political Poetry" (the preface to *Forty Poems Touching on Recent American History*, 1970), in which Bly said that "the writing of political poetry is like the writing of personal poetry, a sudden drive by the poet inward" (quoted in Nelson, 40). Nelson, acknowledging that many critics take the view that *The Light Around the Body* is satire — although he calls it "satire with very little laughter" — categorizes the tone, mood, and effect — indeed, even the structure of the book — as prophetic, its social criticism "based in spiritual values and a vision of transformation" (44-46). For Nelson, then, Bly has created in *The Light Around the Body* a book that insists that "public events have spiritual meaning" and illustrates a "potential for redemption" that "promises revelation" and finally "amounts to an affirmation of faith" (64, 66, 71, 72).

Sugg finds Bly's political doctrine "less important than [his] general moral outrage" and thinks that Bly's knowledge of both poetry and politics provides for his unique preparation among poets to speak out and write during the period of the Vietnam War. Sugg argues that *The Light Around the Body* represents the "best poetry dealing directly with the complex sociopolitical themes of the Vietnam period," but he also feels that Bly's background and preparation "encouraged the over development" of his "public persona" (1986, 38, 41, 42). Even so, Bly's "facing up" to the political test of the Vietnam War is, according to Sugg, an important element in his redefinition of the role of the American poet in the 1960s. In *The Light Around the Body* Bly constantly bases the "historical/political dimension" on the "ontological/psychological dimension" so that the book's poetry "posits the perfection of the outer world upon the improvement of the inner world." Sugg identifies, even though he does not make much of, the three kinds of political poems that Bly writes in *The Light Around the Body* as the poems of "personal experience," the poems of "a satiric visionary," and the poems of an "overwrought partisan." He comes to the conclusion that *The Light Around the Body* ends in "eschatological prophesies" (43, 46, 69).

Davis (1979/80 and 1988) treats Bly's early political and protest poetry in greater detail than most other critics do. Believing that Bly's "notions of 'inwardness' are directly and intricately related to his 'outward' political poems" and to his political and protest positions, Davis, following Bly in using Boehme's notion of the "Two Worlds," analyzes *Silence in the Snowy Fields* and *The Light Around the Body* (whose "contrasts" he finds "conspicuous, but superficial") in the context of Boehme's inner-outer, light-dark dichotomies and attempts to show that, by the end of *The Light Around the Body*, Bly's "aesthetic apocalypticism coincides with traditional Christian eschatology" (1979/80, 75, 83). Davis argues that *The Light Around the Body* makes "a more powerful poetic statement than . . . a political one" even though the poems in "The Vietnam War" section "remain the most specific, the most detailed and the most controversial poetic anti-war statement of the period" (1988, 43, 50). Davis adds, "Finally, then, although *The Light Around the Body* will no doubt be most often remembered for the overt antiwar poems . . . , from the point of view of Bly's developing poetic philosophy it is best seen as a description of the transition from the outer world back into the inner world" (1992, 270). Therefore, by the end of *The Light Around the Body*, and perhaps most conspicuously in "When the Dumb Speak," the final poem of the book, the "dumb" are "both the dead in Vietnam" and the "dead who still live in the psyches of the living" (1988, 65).

"The Teeth Mother Naked at Last," even though it was Bly's most sustained and certainly most bitter antiwar poem, elicited far fewer reviews and critical commentaries than *The Light Around the Body* had. The reason for this was clear enough. Although the poem initially appeared independently, it was subsequently included in Bly's *Sleepers Joining Hands*, a book that had a much more psychological than political focus. Readers and critics seemed confused about how best to treat the poem, and most of them solved this dilemma by not treating it at all.

The reviews and critical responses that "The Teeth Mother Naked at Last" did receive divide rather neatly into several categories. Some critics find the poem "unbearable," a "nightmare," using "the logic of the nightmare" to create a "total experience" (Heffernan, 1971); "disappointing" although taking a "brave and honorable stand" (Naiden, 1971); "organically sick" and "deformed" by didacticism (Reinhold, 1973); a "sort of propaganda" and "often a simple contemplation of unbearable facts" (Libby, 1972); and a "sustained, hate-filled invective against everything in American life that Bly loathed" (Richman, 1986). Other critics call the poem "one of [Bly's] best works to date" (Katz, 1971); a "small masterpiece" (Oates, 1973); "the best poem written during the last decade" (Hyde, 1973); the "long-awaited" poem on the horrors of the Vietnam war (M. D., 1971); the "best examination of our motives during the debacle in Vietnam" (Cavitch, 1973); and, as noted above, the "first poem which attempts political analysis" (Gitlin, 1971).

The most detailed treatments of "The Teeth Mother Naked at Last" are to be found in Howard Nelson, who calls it a "long dramatic diatribe" and a "fiery, smoky sermon" that Bly "largely composed aloud during readings" and in which he transforms the Vietnam War into a "grotesque and powerful poetry" (1984, 51, 87, 92); in Sugg, who calls it the "best postmodern war poem in American literature," Bly's "poetics of apocalypse" in which he is able to "dramatize his message" and tie together his theme of "man's inward, psychospiritual journey" (1986, 73, 76-77); in Davis, who treats it both as "Bly's vision of the apocalypse demanded by man's inhumanity to man as a result of his allegiance to the Teeth Mother" (1981, 267) and as a political satire that "demands a response" (1992a, 2128); and in Kalaidjian, who thinks Bly has "advanced his deep image dissent from Vietnam" in it, and, "reading public history" through his deep image poetics, sees Vietnam, as a "symptom" of the "troubled political unconscious" of America (1989, 132-33).

In his initial analysis of "The Teeth Mother Naked at Last" Davis (1988, 74) summarizes most of the important critical responses to the political protest poetry of this phase of Bly's career:

> "The Teeth Mother Naked at Last," like many of the anti-war poems in *The Light Around the Body*, is didactic and controversial, propagandistic and surreal, but it is also a political, social, and psychological analysis of the malaise of modern society for which the war in Vietnam is only the most immediate and obvious example. In responding subjectively and poetically to the war, in parodying the political propaganda it created, and in tracing its sources through the depths of man's psyche, Bly hopes to awaken himself and his reader to understanding and therapeutic action.

In short, then, these politically overt protest poems of the second phase of Bly's career were, most critics agreed, the "most specific, the most detailed and the most controversial poetic anti-war statement of the period" and also some of "the most stunning political poems in American literature" (Gioia, 1987, 220). Nonetheless, as they also agreed, the poems left critics with a new dilemma: either they had to attempt to deal with Bly's work to date in terms of two at least somewhat seemingly antithetical themes and theses, or they had to try to merge these themes and theses into some coherent system or whole. However, this burden was — as all were willing, even anxious, to affirm — primarily Bly's. That Bly solved it so succinctly in the next phase of his career gave a number of his critics pause — even as they (for the most part) delightfully followed up his leads.

3: The Poetry of Spiritual Energy: *Sleepers Joining Hands*

HAVING FIRMLY ESTABLISHED THE TWO ESSENTIAL THREADS that would be woven, unwoven, and rewoven again into various patterns throughout the fabric of his work, Bly turned toward synthesis in *Sleepers Joining Hands* (1973). In this book he brought together the lyrical thread of *Silence in the Snowy Fields* and the political thread of *The Light Around the Body* and added to them the substantial grounding of the Jungian thought he had been immersing himself in during the past few years. In this sense, once again, Bly took his critics by surprise, just as he had with *The Light Around the Body* — though by now they should have been better prepared for another one of his characteristic leaps.

Three years before *Sleepers Joining Hands* appeared, Bly published a brief statement that he called "Crossing Roads," in which he indicated that he loved the "mysterious lines that cross" in poetry. He described these lines as roads that can "start out in solitude and end in human love"; or begin in "primitive energy," pass "through compassion," and end in "spiritual energy"; or start out as "political energy" and "end in spiritual energy" (1970a, 146). And in an interview given shortly after *Sleepers Joining Hands* appeared, Bly defined perhaps more clearly than anywhere else what this new book aimed at:

> You notice that the psyche is in a state of great energy. Moving with its own immense energy, it becomes equal to the world. Instead of depending on the outer world for support, it begins somehow to create a third world, neither "physical" nor "inner."
>
> It's as if a human being and a badger together would give birth to an angel. Or as if an angel and a tree give birth to a bridge. It's as if a bull woke up one day with so much energy, he ignored the fence-posts and barn-door of his pasture and created Assyria instead. (Fass, 1978, 229)

As these sources indicate, clearly what Bly was about in *Sleepers Joining Hands* was a kind of "road crossing," a situation in which the energy that "has remained inside the psyche" coalesces until it creates a "new substance" (Fass, 1978, 228). Elsewhere, Bly said that life in the twentieth century had gotten "so intense, so soaked with unconscious or half-conscious substance, so deeply impelled by psychic energies desperately attempting to get loose" that it "cannot be understood in any ordinary state of consciousness." Therefore, "poetry gets better only as [the poet] is able to enter states of consciousness that the ordinary 'absorbed' American does not enter" (1969, 5). Apparently Bly intended to suggest that in order to interpret such poetry adequately, critics should also be able to enter similarly unabsorbed states of consciousness.

Bly had now published three books, each of which seemed to go in a different direction. He appeared to be giving his critics warning that they would need to be on their toes to keep dancing with him. Not surprisingly, much of the criticism of *Sleepers Joining Hands* was an attempt to deal with the differences and diversions in Bly's work, and that criticism focused primarily on the differences between *Sleepers Joining Hands* on the one hand and *Silence in the Snowy Fields* and *The Light Around the Body* on the other. Many of Bly's critics — both in their reviews of *Sleepers Joining Hands* and in their more substantial articles, essays, and books — took their leads (as, by now, they had gotten into the habit of doing) from Bly himself.

Like the two earlier books, *Sleepers Joining Hands* was widely reviewed, and there was considerable variety among the almost thirty reviews. Some reviewers attempted to deal with the whole book — the poetry as well as the long prose essay, "I Came Out of the Mother Naked," which constituted the central second section of the book — while others concentrated (sometimes exclusively) on either "The Teeth Mother Naked at Last" or on the essay or on the two together. These differing concentrations led to widely different estimates of the book, since some reviewers tried to treat it retrospectively, others tried to treat it prophetically, and some even tried to treat it both ways simultaneously.

A number of reviewers (Helms, 1977, Piccione, 1973, and Hall, 1973, for instance) see *Sleepers Joining Hands* as Bly's attempt to synthesize or reconcile, and thus cement or integrate, the "inner" and "outer" dichotomous strands of *Silence in the Snowy Fields* and *The Light Around the Body*, although Helms also argues that the poetry fails to reconcile or integrate these dichotomies because Bly himself is so "disintegrated" and because, in *Sleepers Joining Hands*, Bly the poet had chosen to write in the confessional mode that Bly the critic had argued forcefully against and, indeed, had been instrumental in destroying. Helms calls Bly the "critic who most successfully demolished the confessional mode" and views the new book as both "self-conscious" and "sloppy," fragmented in terms of the poetry, although

Helms feels the prose essay succeeds where the poetry fails. For Piccione, *Sleepers Joining Hands* is a "book to rejoice in," a book of balance, a "strangely alive book" in which Bly "resides" "confidently and warmly" both in the meditative mode of *Silence in the Snowy Fields* and in the public mode of *The Light Around the Body* (1973). Hall, calling Bly the "most systematic poet in the United States," calls *Sleepers Joining Hands* the best of Bly's books to date, a book that recapitulates *Silence in the Snowy Fields* and *The Light Around the Body* at the same time that it takes "a further step." For Hall this step "*depends* on the ideas in the prose, and *occurs* in the long title poem that ends the book" (1973, 90).

Other general reviews consider the book pretentious, sententious, or boring and Bly's essay on "mother consciousness" amateurish and poorly written (Anonymous, 1974); or they find it trite or "preachy" (Cooney, 1977); or "dishonest" and "self-deceiving," "shameful even for hate propaganda" (Ramsey, 1974); or audacious and filled with Bly's most conspicuous weakness — "binges" of "excessive rhetoric," though it is a book of unqualified energy and "audacity" (Naiden, 1973); or a "curious mixture of gratuitous statement" and "contrived passiveness" (Chamberlin, 1973; both Naiden and Chamberlin reviewed *Sleepers Joining Hands* together with Bly's *Jumping Out of Bed*, 1973); or "beautifully unified," a "remarkable collection" by a poet who is "reasonable, logical, and extremely persuasive," a poet who, says Oates, has created "one of the most powerful books of any kind I have read recently" (1973).

Still other reviewers (Hyde, 1973, Sternberg, 1973, Zinnes, 1973, Lindquist, 1973/74, and Cooney, 1977) pay special attention to "The Teeth Mother Naked at Last," the long poem at the end of the first section of the book,[1] or to the central prose essay, "I Came Out of the Mother Naked," which an anonymous reviewer (1972) says, proclaimed the "mystery" toward which Bly's poetry had been moving — with implications against which he had tried to "renege." Oppenheimer (1973) considers Bly's essay to be important for the "exposure" of the poetic process it describes; Skelton (1973) discusses Bly's treatment of the "emergence" of mother consciousness over father consciousness in his central essay; Hyde (1973) compares Bly's prose and ideas to the work of D. H. Lawrence, Federico García Lorca, and Henry David Thoreau; Lindquist (1973/74) wonders if Bly is overreacting to the New Criticism, the Vietnam War, and, indeed, "every kind of social injustice"; Walsh (1973) calls Bly the seer of the moment and possibly of the future; Stitt (1973) says that *Sleepers*

---

[1]See chapter two for a more detailed survey of the critical response to "The Teeth Mother Naked at Last."

Joining Hands, especially Bly's essay, is both impressive and also important as a statement on and for the American psyche; Helms, finally, summarizing most of what had been said by others, concludes that Bly has achieved with his prose what he has hoped for in his poetry — the "establishment of community" through "an imaginative reading of the history of his own consciousness" and of the "American culture in which it lives, works, "suffers, and sometimes exults" (1977, 287).

In perhaps the most incisive review of the book, one that attempts to deal equally with each of the various sections and themes individually, Cavitch reviews both Bly the man and his book simultaneously. Arguing that Bly suffers the "ordeal of recent years" as both "American victim and victimizer," a man whose "stomachaches embody the cultural disorder" of the period and a writer who has undertaken the "obligations" of this "vast purpose" (something only the "very greatest writers" can hope to succeed at), Cavitch finds that Bly's book (which has to be "read as a narrative and an argument"), this Whitmanian "large-scale investigation of himself" as the "embodiment of contemporary life," finally fails because of Bly's reliance on some of his "recurrent" weaknesses and the "conventionally happy ending" of the title poem— even though, Cavitch concludes, Bly has succeeded in "partly implicating us in his conclusions" (1973, 2-3).[2]

Bly's statements about his indebtedness to Jung and other psychologists and to the history of depth psychology from Bachofen's *Mother Right* (1861) to the contemporary work of Erich Neumann and James Hillman had been (perhaps purposefully) confusing. Friberg reports that Bly told her he began reading Jung around 1961 but didn't read him seriously until around 1970 and that in the "last few years" (this letter was written in 1976) he had "read him steadily and enthusiastically" (1977, 5, note 1). Howard Nelson says that Bly read Jung "intensively for the first time" in 1969 (1984, xxxiii). Most critics, however, would agree with Sugg, who argues that, throughout his career, Bly has been writing poetry "whose essential form" is "deeply indebted to the terminology and assumptions of evolutionary depth psychology" (1985, 33) and that Jungian psychology is present in Bly's work from the beginning of his career (Sugg, 1986, 31).

In his essay "Developing the Underneath" Bly described Jung's theory of the four "intelligences" and argued that poets should develop their "underneath," their "inferior" functions, which are their "link to all the rest of humanity"; if the "'beneath' is not developed

---

[2]The more substantial criticism, unlike the early reviews of *Sleepers Joining Hands*, sometimes gave the long title poem in the third section of the book special treatment. See below.

then there is no poetry" since "poetry is written with the inferior function." Critics, Bly argued, are notorious for not encouraging "development of the auxiliary powers" but rather "prefer to categorize everyone by the function that first appears," and then they tend to spend the rest of their time "trying to get everyone to stay in his cubbyhole" (1973a, 44-45).

There were two immediate responses to "Developing the Underneath." Louis Simpson disagrees with Bly that feelings have their source in the unconscious. For Simpson, poetry results from thinking about feelings; therefore "there is something unreal about making a division between thought and feeling" (1974, 53). Emma, in a response to this essay and to Bly's slightly earlier essay "The War Between Memory and Imagination" (1973b), feels that Bly has neglected some important historical (and literary) points by "not thinking far enough into the matter" (1974, 53).

"I Came Out of the Mother Naked" is arguably the single most important essay Bly has written — both for *Sleepers Joining Hands* and for the male and female consciousness poems of *The Man in the Black Coat Turns* and *Loving a Woman in Two Worlds*.[3] Since this is such an important essay, it is necessary to indicate, at least briefly, what Bly accomplished in it as well as what his critics accused him of accomplishing. To do so is to point the direction both for all of Bly's future work and for the critical response to it.

Bly began "I Came Out of the Mother Naked" by saying, "I know the poet is not supposed to talk to the reader in the middle of his book" (1973, 29), and then he went on for twenty-one pages to do exactly that. Later he would be the first to admit that his essay was "full of mad generalizations" (1980, 251). According to some of his critics, this essay is Bly's most specific and most detailed summary of his views on Jungian psychology, the theory of archetypes, mother consciousness, father consciousness, and the significance of the "new brain" (see Bly's essay, "The Three Brains" in his *Leaping Poetry*, 1975, 59-67). According to another critic, it is only "a shuffling interlude of notions on parade" (Cavitch, 1973). The consensus seems to be, as Davis indicates, that "I Came Out of the Mother Naked" is "extremely important to an understanding of much of Bly's work" (1988, 79). And, as Howard Nelson says, "Even a reader who begins with a basic skepticism" toward the essay "is likely to emerge . . . feeling that he has been given a rich and useful set of metaphors" — in "some respects more adequate" than the terminology frequently used by psy-

[3]See chapters six and seven for consideration of this essay in terms of Bly's male-female consciousness work and the criticism devoted to it and to these two important later books.

chologists and literary critics — with respect to basic themes and theses behind the poems in this stage of Bly's career (1984, 84-85).

In "Developing the Underneath" and "I Came Out of the Mother Naked" Bly summarized the sources of his psychological themes in *Sleepers Joining Hands* and thus provided the primary background for much of the critical commentary on it — criticism that focused heavily on the mythic and psychological themes (these two threads coming together to create "spiritual energy") that came to climax in this book.

In several important essays, Anthony Libby (1972, 1973, 1984) describes Bly's theory of Great Mother culture (which had been evident as the dominant theory behind some of Bly's recent poems, specifically and most conspicuously "The Teeth Mother Naked at Last") and shows how it develops from both *Silence in the Snowy Fields* and *The Light Around the Body* and how it goes beyond the traditional and the transcendental, as well as the political and the philosophical, to become "prophetic."

Although the role of the prophetic in recent poetry, especially the poetry by Bly and by some of his most immediate contemporaries, is clearly still a critical sidelight, it has become an increasingly important approach to Bly's life and work. And though much of the work on the role of the prophet has been done by scholars in the fields of history, theology, and psychology, several literary critics have attempted to consider contemporary poets and poetry in terms of the prophetic. Altieri (1976), for instance, defines the differences between the seer and the prophet and attempts to show how contemporary poets reconcile these roles. The distinction, he argues, is between the simple presentation of images (done by the seer) and the transformation of those images into myths (the work of the prophet). Bly would seem by this definition to be prophetic.

Libby notes, however, that Bly's "archetypal sociology" in *Sleepers Joining Hands* often "does not fully convince" and that is it necessary and "better" to "accept Bly's explanations as metaphor, his poems as reality," since to see Bly's poetry as "dependent on anyone's theory" — Jung's, Neumann's, or even Bly's own — is "not only to deny [Bly's] belief in the irrational psychic sources of poetry but also to dilute the unique force of his poems" (1972, 86-87). Finally, Libby details how the "struggle for psychic wholeness" is overshadowed by "the drama of mystical union" in the long title poem that concludes *Sleepers Joining Hands* (1984, 175).

In spite of Libby's quite appropriate caution, several critics develop an approach to *Sleepers Joining Hands* from the Jungian point of view and attempt to analyze the correspondences between Bly's theories (especially in his essay "I Came Out of the Mother Naked") and practice (in the title poem) and the parallel or associative relationships and theses put forward by Jung in his voluminous writings. Atkinson, for instance, focuses in detail on the "implicit and continuous parallelism," especially in the title poem, between Bly's work and Jung's schema (1976, 145), showing the ways in which Bly seems to have worked out his accommodation along the lines of his Jungian paradigm and also the lines of his poetic paradigmatic predecessor, Whitman, in the latter's long poem "The Sleepers" (see Davis, 1981, 275). Gitzen argues that *Sleepers Joining Hands* adds "an additional dimension" to the "spiritual quest" that has dominated Bly's work up to this time (1976, 238). Seal, in an extremely interesting and detailed essay, focuses specifically on "Sleepers Joining Hands" (surely one of Bly's most difficult and demanding poems), arguing that Bly is clearly indebted to Jung but that "Sleepers Joining Hands" is "only apparently a Jungian drama," since Bly consciously uses Jung, and unconsciously resists him. Therefore, Seal suggests that Bly's poems will "ultimately be read more for what Bly swept under the rug than for the pattern he wove into it" (1981, 234-35).

Davis, in an essay more broadly conceived than most of the others mentioned above, describes Bly's "poetic, religious, psychological struggle" in *Sleepers Joining Hands* and, through an exercise in "psychic archaeology," attempts to uncover "the substrata of the psyche" in Bly's book and to associate it with Bly's use of myth as expressed by Jung and Neumann and both the "new brain" and the "three brain" theories put forward by Paul MacLean (1949, 1958, 1962, 1964), Arthur Koestler (1968), Charles Fair (1969), and others (1981, 266).[4] However, as Davis says, "since Bly has never been a systematic critic" of his own sources, his readers and his critics are "required to make 'leaps' from one point to another" in his sources, just as Bly himself characteristically does both in his use of his sources and in his poems (272).

Although Kalaidjian's essay (1989) expresses a minority position at the moment, it may well prove to be in the vanguard of the direction future criticism of Bly's work will take, especially in terms of the heavily Jungian oriented material in the middle of his career as well as in the work that focuses on the male-female dichotomy so important to *The Man in the Black Coat Turns* and *Loving a Woman in Two Worlds*. Kalaidjian argues that Bly's specifically "feminine" argument in "I Came Out of the Mother Naked" as well as his mythologically and psychologically oriented poetry in general (in *Sleepers Joining Hands*

---

[4]See Davis, 1981, 257-59, 264-65, and 279-80 note 11 for a more detailed accounting of Bly's groundings in these thinkers and others. Bly's own most explicit comments on the three brains can be found in Bly (1972a, reprinted in 1975 and reprinted and further revised in 1990).

and elsewhere) is flawed since Bly has never fully reflected critically on the sources of his use of the theories of depth psychology (140-41).

The books on Bly develop in greater detail many of the critical approaches to *Sleepers Joining Hands* already noted and add several new suggestions and emphases to the existing arguments. Howard Nelson focuses on Bly's "fundamentally religious" concerns and Whitmanian parallels and, treating Bly primarily as a "poet of the inward life," finds in the book "a poetry of sweep" and "the extravagant gesture" (1984, 74, 76, 79). He suggests that "Sleepers Joining Hands" is a kind of "dream journal," provides a detailed reading of the poem in the context of the larger poetic "dream journal" of Bly's career to this point, and concludes that this poem is Bly's most "ambitious rendering" of his "journey" (100, 112). Like other critics already mentioned, Nelson finds Bly's "heavy and systematic" use of "masculine/feminine terminology" problematical, and he cautions — apparently both Bly and his critics — that "thinking about archetypes can easily skid into thinking in stereotypes" (84).

Sugg, insistently committed to a Jungian approach to Bly, treats *Sleepers Joining Hands* as "psychospiritual myth" and "evolutionary psychology," and his elaborately descriptive and extremely detailed readings of the poems and the prose essay "I Came Out of the Mother Naked" are based on this Jungian orientation. He concludes that in the epic-like "Sleepers Joining Hands" Bly has not only satisfied a "particularly prevalent twentieth-century desire" to "write a long poem" but also created "a veritable theodicy for the twentieth century" through "three major aspects to [his] new voice" in *Sleepers Joining Hands*: the form of the long poem, the centering of both the "dramatic and symbolic personal imagery" around a Jungian paradigm, and "the push through the Jungian archetype toward a spiritual-religious level of meaning" (1985, 88, 102).

Finally, extending his earlier work, Davis provides the most definitive overview of *Sleepers Joining Hands* by treating the book both as a synthesis of the dominant themes and styles of *Silence in the Snowy Fields* and *The Light Around the Body* and as Bly's preparation for work to come. In this sense *Sleepers Joining Hands* is both a "transitional book and . . . a book in transition," and if it "does not contain Bly's most important poetry," it does contain "much of the major theoretical material which makes possible an accurate reading of his most important poetry." Davis traces Bly's major metaphors of the road and the journey (metaphors as old as *Silence in the Snowy Fields*) and other images throughout *Sleepers Joining Hands* and comes to the conclusion that *Sleepers Joining Hands*, compared to *The Light Around the Body*, is finally not a book about "'the light around the body' but a book about the light within" it (1988, 68, 95).

Since Bly had put a little bit of everything into *Sleepers Joining Hands*, it was not surprising that most critics found something to their liking in it. But in the final analysis the critical position on the book's success or failure was far from unanimous. Molesworth, for instance, calls "Sleepers Joining Hands" "Bly's most challenging and most beautiful poem to date" (1979, 120), and Roberson calls the book "perhaps Bly's best volume" to date, a book that synthesizes "all of his interests into one coherent and cogent statement" (1986 xxii). Still, many critics found the book cluttered and confused and had difficulty separating the themes in the prose essay from those in the poetry and organizing them.

No matter what the immediate and ongoing critical commentary found or failed to find in *Sleepers Joining Hands*, it was absolutely clear that this was an important, even climatic, book for Bly on two counts. First, in "I Came Out of the Mother Naked" he put forward the most important theoretical elements of the underpinning and the buttressing of all of his poetry, past, present, and future. Second, he here provided, especially in the two long poems, "The Teeth Mother Naked at Last" and "Sleepers Joining Hands," his earliest, most detailed, and most elaborately worked out poems to date. These, along with the essay placed between them, would support and buttress the rest of his writing.

Even though Bly revised and rewrote some of the poems from *Sleepers Joining Hands* before he included them in his *Selected Poems* (1986) so that, as he said, they "*amount* to new poems" (see Davis, 1988, 96, note 3), Donald Hall is no doubt right when he says of *Sleepers Joining Hands* that it is "the earliest and latest of Bly's works" — that "it had taken this long for [Bly] to use material which leaves him so vulnerable" (1973, 92). This vulnerability evident in *Sleepers Joining Hands* would increasingly become a factor in Bly's future work, and it would become an even greater factor in the criticism of the second half of his career.

4: The Poetry of Prose:
The Morning Glory, This Body Is Made of Camphor and Gopherwood, and *What Have I Ever Lost by Dying?*

BLY'S TURN TO THE PROSE POEM in the middle of his career was, like the "leaps" in his earlier work, accompanied by his own critical apparatus. He argued that the prose poem begins to appear in instances where a culture has moved dangerously close to the abstract, especially when the poetry of that culture has itself gotten "too abstract" (1980, 115). In short, he seemed to be suggesting that prose poems begin to appear at specific times and in specific places as a kind of poetic stay against the extinction of poetry per se in such times and places. Further Bly argued that the poetry that surfaces in such times and places seems to have to make concessions to the prosaic abstractions of those ages by taking on the mantle of the times in order to rescue the times — that is, it becomes prose poetry rather than traditional poetry set down in lines. These notions would have been interesting, even intriguing, from a purely theoretical or critical point of view, but they were even more interesting in light of the fact that following *Sleepers Joining Hands* — a book that seemed to be tending toward abstraction — Bly turned in his next works to the genre of the prose poem. If, as he had argued (1986d, 202), prose poems help to heal the wounds of abstraction and to balance the abstraction that seems imminent in certain periods, then perhaps he was attempting to heal or balance the abstractions of *Sleepers Joining Hands* by turning to the prose poem in *The Morning Glory* (1975) and *This Body is Made of Camphor and Gopherwood* (1977).[1]

Consideration of Bly's recent book of prose poems *What Have I Ever Lost by Dying?* (1992) is included in this chapter rather than being treated separately later on because many of the poems in *What Have I Ever Lost by Dying?* are reprinted from *The Morning Glory* (1975) or

[1]*The Morning Glory* (1975) consists of forty-four prose poems. Fourteen of these poems are newly collected in this edition. The others are reprinted (some of them revised and/or retitled) from two earlier editions of *The Morning Glory* (published in 1969 and 1970 respectively) and from Bly's *Point Reyes Poems* (1974).

from other earlier books: *This Body Is Made of Camphor and Gopherwood* (1977), *This Tree Will Be Here for a Thousand Years* (1979), *The Man in the Black Coat Turns* (1981), *Selected Poems* (1986), and *Ten Poems of Francis Ponge Translated by Robert Bly and Ten Poems of Robert Bly Inspired by Francis Ponge* (1990). Only *The Morning Glory, This Body Is Made of Camphor and Gopherwood, Ten Poems of Francis Ponge Translated by Robert Bly and Ten Poems of Robert Bly Inspired by Francis Ponge* and *What Have I Ever Lost by Dying?* are exclusively collections of prose poems. The other books from which prose poems are included consist primarily of poems in lines. However, since Bly has reprinted many of the earlier prose poems (some of them extensively revised and/or retitled) in *What Have I Ever Lost by Dying?*, it seems best to consider all of the prose poems together even though in some ways this violates a strict chronological sequence, especially if one considers each new revision of an earlier poem as a new poem, as Bly often does.

Bly has frequently commented on the "genreless genre" of the prose poem (neither prose nor poetry alone and both prose and poetry together), and his remarks are important in the ongoing criticism of the form, for their bearing on his own practice of the genre, and because a number of his critics have considered them in their criticism of his prose poems.

If Bly's comments on prose and poetry, if not prose poetry itself, were vague, unsystematic, and often seemingly contradictory in the early years (see, for instance, Bly 1960, 1960a, 1961, 1962a, and 1963), they became more definitive and systematic when he began to write more prose poems. In "What the Prose Poem Carries With It" (1977) Bly said that prose poems absorb details better than lined poems, allow the poem to give equal and individual space to many "separate events," permit a return to "original perceptions," help to make immediate intimacy, celebrate "what takes place only once," and are spoken by a man or woman "talking not before a crowd but in a low voice to someone he is sure is listening" (44-45). In another essay he associated prose poems with the "seeing" poems of Rainer Maria Rilke and the "object" poems of Francis Ponge and called them poems that "long" to "give honor to objects." When poems give honor to objects, Bly said, the object "links with the human psyche," and "the unconscious passes into the object and returns" (1980a, 106, 107). Bly quotes Ponge: "Hope . . . lies in a poetry through which the world so invades the spirit of man that he becomes almost speechless, and later reinvents a language." In this sense, poets "are the ambassadors of the silent world," sinking to the "darkness of logos" until "they reach the level of ROOTS" (1972, 108). In one of his most useful statements on the prose poem, Bly said, "I write prose poems when I long for intimacy." He went on to say that "the prose poems I write belong to the tradition of Jiménez and Francis Ponge, and pay respect to their love of minute particulars." In these poems, "form agrees to a tension between private spontaneity and the hard impersonal" (1985a, 17-18). Finally, Bly said, "prose poems flow as rivers flow, following gravity around a rock" (1986, 143).

Bly's most definitive statement of his theory and practice of the prose poem, however, was "The Prose Poem as an Evolving Form," the final essay in his *Selected Poems*; in it he summarized his earlier, more scattered, comments. At the end of this essay he said, "The fact that no critics have yet laid out formal standards for the prose poem is a blessing" (1986, 204). Even if this is so, a number of poets and critics have made important statements about prose poems historically as well as in individual poetic practice, particularly Bly's. A brief summary of these views is in order here.

Benedikt, in the first substantial American book on the prose poem from an international perspective, describes, details, and anthologizes this "international" poetic form that, although new to the United States, has been practiced "by major poets abroad" for several centuries (1976, 39). Benedikt says that T. S. Eliot, with his "incomparably influential writings" that are "fundamentally English-based" and his "anti-internationalist critical approach" — especially evident in his "most influential" essay, "Tradition and the Individual Talent," in which Eliot asserts that "every nation . . . has not only its own creative, but its own critical turn of mind" — had put American poetry into a kind of "psychic slavery" from which it did not break away until the 1960s. Benedikt argues that this new freedom, made possible by Bly and others, leads "directly to the rediscovery of the prose poem in America today" (40-41). He identifies five essential properties of the prose poem: "the need to attend to the priorities of the unconscious" and to its "particular logic, unfettered" by the "interruptions of the line break"; an "accelerated use of colloquial" and other everyday speech patterns; "a visionary thrust"; a sense of humor that "registers the fluctuating motions of consciousness"; and "a kind of enlightened doubtfulness, or hopeful skepticism" (48-49). Finally, Benedikt argues that Bly's essay "Looking for Dragon Smoke" (1972b and in *Leaping Poetry: An Idea with Poems and Translations*, 1975) "bids fair to become as central to our time" as "Tradition and the Individual Talent" is to Eliot's; that Bly, "far from merely subtracting old techniques from poetry" (as Eliot had), has called for and, indeed, initiated a new technique in American poetry in his "break-through toward the prose poem" (41-42).

Other critics and scholars elaborate on these ideas about the significance of the prose poem for American poetry and for Bly's poetry particularly. Mills describes the prose poem as a "strange, marvelous poetic form" that "possesses great flexibility and almost no restrictions"; that is "complementary" to the "free, variable lines" of Bly's other, earlier poems; that is "elastic and accommodating"; and that may be lyric, dramatic, descriptive, narrative, "fabulistic," anecdotal, or "some combination of these, or something else entirely." He points out that "each poet who takes up the prose poem does so for particular reasons" and that these reasons both influence and help to give that poet's work its "singular, distinctive character" (1976/77, 37, 38, 46).

Fredman deals with the "paradoxical act of writing poetry in prose" by arguing that the American poet, beginning with a sense of alienation, attempts to create "a space of permission" with the world. He further argues that prose poetry is "central" to our time; that it is "critically serious"; and that it works to create a climactic "moment in which poetry, philosophy, and criticism begin to coalesce" (1983, 2, 6, 10). Russell Edson, himself a prolific and important writer of prose poems, argues for a crucial distinction between poetry and prose. According to Edson, "Time flows *through* prose and *around* poetry. . . . And it is the two edges of contradictory time touching . . . that creates the central metaphor of the prose poem" (1976, 322, 324).[2]

Finally, in his history of prose poetry, Monroe finds in Bly one of the most influential of the practitioners and proponents of the prose poem and argues that Bly's work "provides occasion for coming to terms with the genre's function in the context of contemporary aesthetic and political conditions." Furthermore, he says, Bly's turn to the form of the prose poem "coincides, somewhat surprisingly given the prose poem's past norm-breaking function, its history as a genre of revolt, with an increasing depoliticization of Bly's own work" (1987, 41). Therefore, although Bly's prose poems "evidence a certain domestication of the genre" that allows him to "relate rather cozily to an already acquired audience," they also "participate in the genre's profound expression of utopian longing" and thus reject the "subversive historical function" of the tradition for a "more mystical and religious" approach (41-42, 281, 282).

The reviews of Bly's collections of prose poems were considerably varied. Although *The Morning Glory* received fewer reviews than Bly's previous books had, the reviewers were in greater agreement on it than they had been on most of his earlier collections. A number of them found suggestions of renewal, return, and rebirth in the book, and they emphasized the visionary, apocalyptic, and ecstatic elements of these prose poems. Many of the reviews are brief, largely descrip-

---

[2]Also see Edson (1975). Cf. Bly (1986): "Prose poems flow as rivers flow, following gravity around a rock." (143).

tive, and generally favorable (Skinner, 1973; Bedell, 1975; Anonymous, 1975; Anonymous, 1976); others are mixed in their responses to the genre itself and/or to Bly's prose poems specifically (Lattimore, 1976; Dresbach, 1978); one anonymous reviewer (1976a) thinks that Bly has found "new poetic powers" in *The Morning Glory*. These poems, then, most of the reviewers agree, are important new poems in an important genre that is new to America. They are, in short, poems not to be missed.

There were several more substantive reviews of *The Morning Glory*. Plumly calls Bly "our Thoreau" and a "visionary of detail" in the "small, unattended moment[s]" so many of these poems explore. He finds the book building to "revelations" — indeed, to "complete spiritual constructs" (1975). Davis sees the book as Bly's poetic attempt to escape the abstraction of the aftermath of the Vietnam War and, thus, through the prose poem, find "a way of maintaining the possibility of poetry in an age about to abandon it." He calls *The Morning Glory* "Bly's most specific version of his personal apocalyptic" and points out that it ends with two poems about new beginnings (1977). Mersmann finds *The Morning Glory* the climax of Bly's career to date — a collection of poems that is "more free, spontaneous, excited, and sensuous than any of his previous work"; poetry in which Bly, through the exercise of his "tremendously athletic imagination," has managed to "ecstatically rediscover" "profound correspondences" in the world; a book in which Bly has "finally gone out of his mind and come to his senses" (1977).

There were more reviews of *This Body Is Made of Camphor and Gopherwood* than of *The Morning Glory*, and they were more mixed than those that greeted the earlier collection. Some reviewers even take positive and negative positions simultaneously. Reviewers find *This Body Is Made of Camphor and Gopherwood* "overweight and pretentious" and thus "not mysticism but solipsism" (Cotter, 1978); "hallucinatory" in the ways in which Bly has attempted to "write down" what it is like "to be alive" (Kenner, 1978); a book filled with poems of "undeniable intensity and candor," though the poems do not rival the greatest poems in the genre of prose poetry from an international perspective (Fuller, 1978); a "blah-book," filled with "moony questions and muzzy pantheism" (Anonymous, 1977); or a "beautiful" book with deep images resonating with their own "stillness" (Ringold, 1978).

One of the most substantive reviews of *This Body Is Made of Camphor and Gopherwood* describes the book as "emphatically a book of deep religious longing" combining a "prophetic quality" with a "grandiose purpose bordering on battiness" and concludes that Bly wants "nothing less than to be a saint" (Dacey, 1978). Davis argues that these are "crucial transitional poems" (1992) "of the life and death of consciousness" that "plumb the soul," and deal with matters of life and death in such a way that they "make life and death matter" (1977a). In two separate reviews, Molesworth holds that in *This Body Is Made of Camphor and Gopherwood* Bly has extended his vision beyond the ranges established in the prose-poems of *The Morning Glory*; that there is a sense of "rightness" that neatly combines the "expectations of prose" with the "advantages of poetry"(1978); and that this "decisive change" in Bly's work, these poems filled with "nodes of psychic energy" that are overtly poems of "religious vision," are Bly's attempts to use "this body" as an ideal and universal symbol and thereby to "domesticate the sublime" (1978a). (Roberson [1986, 316] suggests that the earlier Molesworth review is "strangely awkward"; it is as if Molesworth, usually one of Bly's most perceptive critics, could not "identify something bothersome" in this book, which he clearly respects.)

What Have I Ever Lost by Dying? has been out only for a few months as this book goes to press, and to date there have been no substantial reviews of it. The early notices, primarily in publishers' periodicals and library journals, are brief and do not consider the book in the context of Bly's other books of prose poems, though more than two-thirds of *What Have I Ever Lost by Dying?* is made up of prose poems reprinted (many of them much revised, some more than once) from *Point Reyes Poems, The Morning Glory, This Body Is Made of Camphor and Gopherwood, The Man in the Black Coat Turns, Selected Poems,* and *Ten Poems of Francis Ponge Translated by Robert Bly and Ten Poems of Robert Bly Inspired by the Poems of Francis Ponge.*

The early short notices, however, may in some senses indicate the directions that the more substantial reviews and critical responses to this book will take. They call the poems "joyous, inspired meditations that demonstrate Bly's talent for conveying in the simplest language the richness and complexity of the universe around us" (Poole, 1992); poems that "go down easily, like a long drink of water" and are "refreshing and clarifying," filled with "imaginative leaps and resonant visions" (Seaman, 1992); "luminous" descriptions of the "metaphysics of living and dying that illustrate the ways in which life and death are "synchronous" (Anonymous, 1992); "memorable" poems, clear expressions of the "receptivity" achieved in solitude by this poet who "can meditate a stone into being" (Chang, 1993). On the negative side, Allen views the book as the work of one "who has inspired more than his share of foolishness" but who here, "surprisingly," "manages to capture . . . many little things often left unnoticed" as he passes the objects of his poetry "through the filter of the Men's Movement philosophy"[3] — even if, finally, he "too frequently becomes himself," with the result that the poems sometimes "disintegrate into diary entries" (1992).

The majority of the articles on Bly's prose poems, whether focusing on them as a genre or primarily on one specific collection, are applicable to the several collections of prose poems. Libby argues that the prose poems of *This Body Is Made of Camphor and Gopherwood* have a somewhat forced or artificial beauty as a result of their "visionary quality" and the "sacrifice of the visible for the dream" in them. In contrast, he suggests, in the prose poems of *The Morning Glory* (and also many of the poems in *This Tree Will Be Here for a Thousand Years*), the "visible and invisible are described together," which makes for a "resonant clarity" (1981, 52-53). Likewise, Nelson says that "the prose poem feels distinctly different in the two books" (1984, 167).

Among the critical articles that attempt to deal with the entire canon of Bly's prose poems published over the years, Molesworth provides the most succinct summary of Bly's slow and carefully "unobtrusive" mastery of the prose poem, arguing that Bly's "seeing has seldom been more precise" than it is in these "self-effacing" "celebrations" of "private sensibility" moving from one "tack-sharp" detail to another, with metaphors and similes that "clear their own ground as they go" (1979, 119-24).

In several separate articles, Mills considers Bly's prose poems in considerable detail. He points out early on — before most critics had begun to consider the prose poems either individually or in the context of Bly's canon — that Bly's use of the prose poem, especially in *The Morning Glory* and *Old Man Rubbing His Eyes* (1975) which "emerge from the same primal ground" of Bly's imagination, complements his early work in lined poems, especially the "Six Winter Privacy Poems" of *Silence in the Snowy Fields,* and that his work in both genres represents a "substantial accomplishment" both for Bly and "for the prose poem in America" (1976/77, 46). Mills later traces the unique organic development of Bly's theory and practice of prose poetry and argues that Bly's prose poems come to climax as a "fine coherent achievement" (1981, 49).

Harris sees Bly's use of the prose poem as "accommodating" his "stance as a subjectivist who wishes to grasp the universal by pene-

[3]This is obviously a reference to Bly's work with men's groups during the past decade, and to work that he focuses on in his best-selling book, *Iron John: A Book About Men* (1990), and its recent "companion" volume, *The Rag and Bone Shop of the Heart: Poems for Men* (1992), which Bly edited with James Hillman and Michael Meade. For more on this side of Bly's career, see below and also the Appendix, *"Iron John: A Book About Men* and the Critics."

trating the particular" (1990, 15). In another essay she considers his prose poems in terms of their relationship to "female consciousness," the uses of intuition, and "psychic integration" and suggests that, in certain of these poems, Bly constructs a "mythology of human experience" (1981).

Davis, likewise, analyzes Bly's prose poems in several individual essays (1982, 1984). He catalogues some of the most important historical parallels to Bly's prose poetry as well as the personal backgrounds to these poems in Bly's earlier work (both poetry and prose) as prelude to a detailed reading of a number of the individual prose poems. Then he attempts to show how Bly, in using the genre of the prose poems so effectively (and thus making it more usable for others), has opened up new possibilities for poetry "in an age which might well have been about to abandon it" (1984, 148).

The book-length treatments of Bly's work in the prose poem follow up some of these suggestions and add several new ones. Nelson provides a brief survey of the history of the prose poem as genre; considers Bly's critical comments on prose poetry in relation to his poetic practice; details Bly's indebtedness to both Francis Ponge and Rainer Maria Rilke in terms of "kinship" associations; discusses the dual presences of "death and animals" in many of these poems (especially those in *The Morning Glory*) and the often abrupt shifts from the "creaturely to the visionary" in them; sees the prose poem (especially in *This Body Is Made of Camphor and Gopherwood*) as a kind of "action writing" for various "currents of energy"; and analyzes some of Bly's individual prose poems (1984, 145, 151, 172). For Nelson, Bly's work in this genre is divided between the "intense observation" and the "irrepressible subjectivity and intuitiveness" of *The Morning Glory* and the flamboyance and "audacity" of *This Body Is Made of Camphor and Gopherwood*, which, he argues, is an "attempt to name energy and flow themselves" (134, 171).

Sugg concentrates on Bly's prose poems — that "uncommon hybrid" of prose and poetry — and his other work of the 1970s, poetry and prose (especially *News of the Universe: Poems of Twofold Consciousness*, 1980, in which Bly's critical essays are often directly applicable to his poetry of this period), with reference to Bly's "attraction" to "*Gott-natur*," "divine instinctuality," and the "twofold consciousness" typical of the prose poem (1986, 104-5). Sugg finds a "spiritual theme" in both *The Morning Glory* and *This Body Is Made of Camphor and Gopherwood*, but he feels that this emphasis is stronger in *This Body Is Made of Camphor and Gopherwood*, "Bly's book of the holiness of the body." This theme, along with the other major theme of the book, the "psychospiritual nature of the human imperative to pursue the inward road of self-exploration," could, he argues, be seen most fully in the central poem of the book, "The Origin of the Praise of God," the only poem from *This Body Is Made of Camphor and Gopherwood* that Bly included in *News of the Universe: Poems of Twofold Consciousness*, thus showing, according to Sugg, "its significance to [Bly's] theory of consciousness" (100, 109, 111).

Davis, using Bly's suggestion that prose poems appear when an age moves dangerously close to the "abstract" and seeing Bly as the paradigm of the poet of his period in literary history, argues that in attempting to "define the age" by defining himself in the prose poems of *The Morning Glory* and *This Body Is Made of Camphor and Gopherwood*, Bly is returning both imagistically and thematically to his own beginnings (to *Silence in the Snowy Fields* and the "Six Winter Privacy Poems" of *Sleepers Joining Hands*) in an attempt to begin again. Although this shift in form here in the middle of his career is conspicuous, it is not as important as the return that these prose poems effect thematically. After defining the significance of the history and practice of the prose poem (and of Bly's individual history and use of the form), Davis analyzes the poems in both *The Morning Glory* and *This Body Is Made of Camphor and Gopherwood* in an attempt to document Bly's unique contribution to the genre and to show how Bly extended his "basically 'religious' theme" from *The Morning Glory* into the "realm of the ecstatic" in *This Body Is Made of Camphor and Gopherwood*. Bly's prose poems, Davis concludes, "rise up to a body beyond the physical body" in an attempt to "define and finally to name" what is, outside of the poetry itself, "unnamable" (1988, 117, 128).

Harris's 1992 book reprints as her chapter on Bly's prose poetry her 1990 article mentioned above. After surveying and summarizing some of the existing criticism on the history of the prose poem and Bly's contribution to that history, Harris finds that Bly's subjective approach to the form in his own poetry is an attempt to "grasp the universal by penetrating the particular" (87). She concentrates her analysis of the genre on Bly's poem "Walking Swiftly" (the opening poem of *This Body Is Made of Camphor and Gopherwood*) and comes to the conclusion that the "seamlessness" and "suppleness" of Bly's prose poetry corresponds to the "holistic notion of the universe which inspires him" (101-2).

It is not surprising, then, that these prose poems of Bly's middle career elicited a considerable variety of critical responses. What was even more immediately obvious here at this stage of his career, however, was that Bly seemed increasingly willing and able to provide his critics (both in his poetry and in his own criticism) with the means with which to read him, even if this did not assume that all of his critics would thereby be more sympathetic to such critical suggestions or to the poems associated with them, as the widely divergent responses to his future work would show.

5: The Poetry from the Deep
of the Mind: *This Tree Will Be Here
for a Thousand Years*

WHEN HE PUBLISHED HIS FIRST BOOK, *Silence in the Snowy Fields*, in 1962, Bly introduced his poetry of the "new imagination," poetry that depended upon "deep images" as its signature and for it significance. This early poetry was well received and widely admired and imitated, even though Bly himself had quickly incorporated and then gone beyond these early deep image poems in his subsequent books. Therefore, it was somewhat surprising (although not altogether out of character for Bly) that, with *This Tree Will Be Here for a Thousand Years* (1979), he returned to the manner and mode of *Silence in the Snowy Fields*, seemingly suddenly if not completely arbitrarily.

This Tree Will Be Here for a Thousand Years was divided into two sections. In the first, Bly reprinted the twenty poems originally published as *Old Man Rubbing His Eyes* (1975); to the second he added an additional twenty-four poems. The book was introduced by a prefatory essay entitled "The Two Presences," in which Bly discussed both what he had attempted to accomplish in these poems and the way in which they were related to his earlier "snowy fields" poems.[1] He said that the poems in *This Tree Will Be Here for a Thousand Years* "try to achieve 'two presences'" both by "adopting the line with simple syntax" and by the thematic attempt to merge "two separate energies: my own consciousness" and "a second consciousness" that he described, following Lucretius, as "the tear inside the stone," "an energy circling downward . . . moving slowly around apple trees or stars." He went on to say that the poems in *This Tree Will be Here for a Thousand Years* "form a volume added to *Silence in the Snowy Fields*; the two books make one book" (Bly, 1979a, 9-11). In the prefatory note to the selection of poems from *Silence in the Snowy Fields* and *This Tree Will Be*

[1]Bly had frequently referred to his snowy fields poems. See, for instance, his interview with Peter Martin (Bly, 1980, 121-22), in which he said, "I write what you call 'snowy fields' poems without pause, maybe eight or nine a year." Critics have frequently noted this reference and other similar ones and have often referred to the poems of *Silence in the Snowy Fields* and *This Tree Will Be Here for a Thousand Years* as Bly's "snowy fields" poems.

Here for a Thousand Years in his *Selected Poems* (1986), Bly called these poems poems of "a deep of the mind" (26) and said,

> I worked in the *Snowy Fields* poems to gain a resonance among the sounds, and hidden below that there is a second resonance between the soul and a loved countryside, . . . the countryside of my childhood. . . . I wrote a hundred or so of these poems during the three years from 1958 to 1961 . . . and chose forty-four of them for *Silence in the Snowy Fields.* . . . A second group was published under the title *This Tree Will Be Here for a Thousand Years*, in 1979, and a third group will be published later. (27)

These preliminary considerations provide a pertinent and necessary prolegomenon to a survey of the criticism of *This Tree Will Be Here for a Thousand Years* since even Bly's casual comments, to say nothing of his more specific critical commentaries and his theories of literary history and contemporary poetic practice, had become increasingly important to the criticism that his own work received. If it is the case that every writer teaches his critics how to read his work, Bly seemed to have taken his readers and his critics yet another step in this direction by teaching them how to do the criticism which was necessary in order to read his work "correctly" and effectively. Indeed, as Richman points out, criticism of poetry in general during the 1970s "underwent a drastic change, thanks in part to Bly's theories. . . . An entire way of writing about poetry was quickly becoming obsolete, and it was Bly who had played a major role in drafting the blueprint of its destruction." And regardless of whether one were to view this association between the poetry and the criticism positively or negatively (Richman calls it Bly's "anti-critical" criticism, meant to accompany his "anti-poetic poetry"), it was an important influence on the criticism of the period and on the criticism of Bly's work during this period in particular (1986, 43).

The reviews of *This Tree Will Be Here for a Thousand Years*, like the reviews of *This Body Is Made of Camphor and Gopherwood*, were mixed. A number of the reviewers used Bly's preface, "The Two Presences," as a springboard for their comments on the book. Carruth (1980) calls Bly's theory of the two consciousnesses "Swedenborgian nonsense" that "saps" the mind; but, even so, he finds himself responding favorably to many of the poems in the book. He says, "Sometimes it is good, better than good, to guard oneself and still be caught." Williamson (1980) argues that the premise of the two presences is Bly's attempt to free his poetry from the "overtly intellectual" content and the "doctrinaire religiosity" it had developed; the "sadness" of these poems relieves Bly of the "burden of Messianic overconfidence" and allows him to return to the terrain of *Silence in the Snowy Fields*. For more specific and detailed comments on the relationship between "The Two Presences" and *This Tree Will Be Here for a Thousand Years*, see Stitt (1980, 663-66 and 1992, 287-88) for a negative view and Davis (1988, 32-39) for a more positive one. Stitt, thinking of Bly's influence on contemporary American poetry — and in spite of his reservations about this particular book — calls Bly the Ezra Pound of the contemporary period. For Stitt, this "uneven book," marred by Bly's preface, contains many "good poems" which, if they are not original in "vision" or "technique," are nonetheless "well-written" and "pleasurable" (1992, 289).

Other reviewers argue that the poems in *This Tree Will Be Here for a Thousand Years* are "hermetic and elitist" (Garrison, 1979); seldom successful (Saucerman, 1981); attempts to "overcharge" with "psychic significance" moments that ultimately cannot justify such attention (Cotter, 1980); an "impressive gathering" of poems possessing a "rare simplicity" and providing a clear and compassionate vision of the "human predicament" (Anonymous, 1979) — all of which make *This Tree Will Be Here for a Thousand Years* Bly's best book yet (Anonymous, 1979a) and "an important event" (Janik, 1980) on the landscape of contemporary American poetry.

Since *This Tree Will Be Here for a Thousand Years* contained the twenty poems originally published in *Old Man Rubbing His Eyes*, it is worth mentioning here the several independent reviews that *Old Man Rubbing His Eyes* received. Garrison (1975) heralds Bly's gifts for the intuitive and "subliminal"; Mills (1976/77), referring to Bly's poem "To Live" (Bly 1975a, 29), calls these poems "floating" poems; M. K. S. (1978) suggests that the poems involve Bly's readers in his visionary experiences; and an anonymous reviewer (1975a) describes the Oriental sense of inner meaning that arises out of Bly's use of even the simplest observations in these poems. Schjotz-Christensen (1976) argues that in *Old Man Rubbing His Eyes* Bly has confronted death with a greater sense of urgency and imagination than anyone else in contemporary American poetry; this "psychic openness" in the face of death (which Schjotz-Christensen thinks is at the core of Bly's imagination) provides a "strangely evocative testament to the resiliency of [Bly's] lyrical imagination."

The most detailed and caustic of the negative responses to *This Tree Will Be Here for a Thousand Years* was an ad hominem attack on Bly and the poems by Weinberger (1979), who calls Bly an apostle of Romanticism and a "windbag, a sentimentalist, a slob in the language" and calls poetry in the present age a "useless pleasantry, largely ignored" — a fortunate circumstance, according to

Weinberger, since this "utterly safe" and "cozily irrelevant" poet's success in the literary community, especially with younger poets, is less disheartening in a time like the present than it might have been at some other more "important" period in literary history.

Several critics responded negatively to this review. Wesling refers to Weinberger's "memorably brutal attack" on Bly as a "flinty account, unusual . . . for . . . being entirely negative," even though, as he points out, "Bly himself had been a fierce reviewer," and since he had encouraged young writers to criticize established writers, he "wouldn't want his own work to be exempt" (1981a, 447). Nelson calls Weinberger's review "probably the most vitriolic" that Bly had received and points out that, beyond the fact that it represents "one extreme of opinion," it also serves as a kind of primer for the ways in which Bly's work is "likely to be oversimplified and distorted by those hostile to his ends, means, or personality" (1984, 186).

Perhaps the considerable variety of the early responses to *This Tree Will Be Here for a Thousand Years* can best be seen in the drastically different responses to two lines from "Women We Never See Again" (Bly, 1979, 41):

> Sometimes when you put your hand into a hollow tree
> you touch the dark places between the stars.

Weinberger says that this "remark" "might be charming if uttered by a 6-year old" (504). Carruth, on the other hand, says, "Not many of Bly's readers have done that, I imagine, but I . . . *have* done it. I'm damned if he isn't right (1980, 79). Later critics also focus on these lines and come to somewhat different conclusions: Nelson calls "such intuitive moments . . . perhaps the principal reward of *This Tree Will Be Here for a Thousand Years*" (1984, 187); Kramer (1983) calls the hollow in the tree "a site of sudden epiphany" (459) and cites the lines in the conclusion to his argument of the thesis of much of Bly's work. He writes,

> Bly's aim in *This Tree Will Be Here for a Thousand Years* is to find a severe simplicity by submitting attention to a drastic discipline. He looks into his privileged landscape to single out two or three objects, not necessarily related ones, which animate each other or their horizon merely by existing together. The objects all belong to the life of rural work and its seasonal imperatives; they are all somehow innocent; and they are all sanctified by their participation in the primary mystery of natural space: "Sometimes when you put your hand into a hollow tree /you touch the dark places between the stars." (454).

In the context of Bly's canon to date, and specifically in terms of its association with *Silence in the Snowy Fields*, several critics see *This Tree Will Be Here for a Thousand Years* as an "obvious effort to conciliate" readers who have "grown impatient" with his work (Richman, 1986); or as a "sentimental journey" that self-consciously repeats the manner and mode of *Silence in the Snowy Fields* (Gioia, 1987).

Bly has recently published a new edition of *This Tree Will Be Here for a Thousand Years* (1992). This is a major revision of the book: thirty-four of the original forty-four poems have been revised, (twenty-two of them significantly, including, in most of these instances, title changes); "The Two Presences" preface has been almost completely revised away, literally reduced to a single mechanically descriptive paragraph; the section groupings, the number of sections, and the ordering of the poems throughout the book have been considerably changed around. In short, this new version essentially constitutes a new book. To date there have been no reviews or critical notices of the new edition of *This Tree Will Be Here for a Thousand Years*. It is as if the reviewers and the critics have not yet thought that there could be something new in a "revised book." Given Bly's continuous, even increasingly obsessive, penchant for revision, however, this is a dangerous oversight.

Only a few substantial articles were devoted primarily or exclusively to the first edition of *This Tree Will Be Here for a Thousand Years*, but each of them is important. Wesling considers the book in tandem with Bly's collection of interviews, *Talking All Morning* (1980), published a year later. He calls *Talking All Morning* "indispensable"; a book that is "moral, prophetic, eloquently self-suspicious"; and, finally, a "highly persuasive cultural statement whose leading idea is that the American commonwealth wishes to suppress ecstasy and concentration, which are the performal sources of poetry" (1981, 147-48, 153). Even if Bly is "often wrong," Wesling says, his "crazy wisdom" has made him "more consistently productive than any other commentator on recent American culture and poetry." Wesling finds Bly's book of poems "less strong" than his "book of talk." Focusing heavily on prosody, the poetic forms of the poems themselves, and the use of image as "essence," he attempts to evaluate Bly's "magnificent poetics of essence and effect," though he feels that the poems remain incomplete because of Bly's inadequate attention to form — "he wants details of the world in his poetics, not details of language" — a lack of attention that is the result, according to Wesling, of Bly's more specific thematic concern with "spiritual advances" in his work (149-50).

Kramer, in an incisive and important piece on *This Tree Will Be Here for a Thousand Years*, takes an approach almost opposite to the one put forward by Wesling. Kramer argues that Bly's poetry in *This Tree*

Will Be Here for a Thousand Years "depends on a poetic rather than on an esoteric context" and has its source in the kind of "primary truth" that is "known to intuition and expressible in myth"; as such, it is a poetry of "immanence" and is "written to be a fragment of a lost, privileged presence"; it is a poetry that is concerned with "things" more than with "words" and that "moves by groping forward metonymically" (1983, 448, 449). Kramer calls *This Tree Will Be Here for a Thousand Years* a book of "striking austerity" (450). With *Silence in the Snowy Fields*, he thinks it is "arguably the best measure" of Bly's work to date. Working his analysis of the book into the terms of Bly's dichotomy in "The Two Presences," Kramer argues that the poems in *This Tree Will Be Here for a Thousand Years* are "constantly envisioning things at a vanishing point" and that they remain consistent in refusing to balance a noticeable "tilt toward desolation" (458, 459). *This Tree Will Be Here for a Thousand Years* thus "carries the austere conviction" of a "backward look that forgives what it cannot recover" and achieves the kind of "somber intensity" absent from Bly's work since *Silence in the Snowy Fields* (461). Rehder (1992) calls Kramer's definition of the typical Bly poem as an example of a poem of immanence as "unsatisfactory" as the earlier use of the term deep image to describe Bly's work.

Harris's essay (1990a; reprinted in Harris, 1992, with minor variations), the most exhaustive to date on *This Tree Will Be Here for a Thousand Years*, provides a background for the poems in various interrelated disciplines, including philosophy, psychology, epistemology, theology, and literary theory — especially postmodernist, poststructuralist, male-female consciousness, and systems theory. Relying on LeClair (1987), Wilden (1980), and others, Harris summarizes the contributions of a number of thinkers: Morris Berman (1981) with respect to the historical backgrounds of the various pertinent disciplines; Fritjof Capra (1975, 1982), who provides a synopsis and synthesis of physics and Eastern mysticism; Gregory Bateson (1972) and his anthropological studies on mind-body relationships; and Ludwig von Bertalanffy (1968), whose general systems theories are important to the systems theory background. Harris also compares Bly's essay "The Two Presences" to J. E. Lovelock's chromatographic studies and their relationship to Gaia, which Lovelock (1987, vii) defines as "the Earth's living matter, air, oceans, and land surface [that] form a complex system which can be seen as a single organism" and have "the capacity to keep our planet a fit place for life" (quoted in Harris, 1990, 63-64).

In addition, Harris argues that Bly's "pronouncements," such as his "The Two Presences" preface and other comments (in his 1970b interview, for instance), open him up to charges that he is naïve or, even worse, out of touch with the "major intellectual currents of his culture." Harris then attempts to show how variations on such charges occur and recur throughout much of the Bly criticism of the 1980s, which, she argues, derives either from the poststructuralist "insistence on the indeterminacy of language" or from the postmodernist "predilection for irony and self-reflexiveness" (434).

These or similar charges were brought against Bly by Altieri, who chides him for evading responsibility for his "rhetorical means" (1980, 206); by Holden, who finds Bly's poems deficient since they take "too literally" the "epistemological demands inherent in their formal analogues" and thus, through their use of the "fallacy of imitative form," revert to a "primeval mode of consciousness" (1983, 20-21); and by Breslin, who feels that Bly has "repudiated that part of his mind that would permit him to become self-conscious about" his work (1984, 180).

Harris concedes that, from these basic prejudices and perspectives, Bly's poetry "appears hopelessly mystical and quasi-religious"; but, she argues, given the newer critical approaches summarized above — which "echo Bly's utterance[s]" in such a way that the poet, rather than being an "inheritor" of these "new conceptual paradigm[s]," should more properly be seen as a "participant" in their "development" — Bly's work is neither naïve nor out of touch with its age but precisely the opposite on both counts (1990a, 435, 437, 439). For Harris, Bly's "universe" is "intuitive, integrative, perceptive, empathic"; it is, finally, "a participatory universe" (Harris, 1992, 79) that Bly has created between himself and most of his readers if not all of his critics.

Each of the book-length studies of Bly treated *This Tree Will Be Here for a Thousand Years* in the context of his other works, most frequently in tandem with, or as a sequel to, *Silence in the Snowy Fields*.

Nelson (1984) associates *This Tree Will Be Here for a Thousand Years* with *Silence in the Snowy Fields* and *Old Man Rubbing His Eyes* and with Bly's next major book, *The Man in the Black Coat Turns* (1981). Sugg (1986) deals with *This Tree Will Be Here for a Thousand Years* in the context of Bly's work throughout the whole of the 1970s. Davis (1988), like Nelson, associates *This Tree Will Be Here for a Thousand Years* with *Old Man Rubbing His Eyes* and then considers it structurally, formally, and thematically in parallel with *Silence in the Snowy Fields*. For Nelson, *This Tree Will Be Here for a Thousand Years* is a "paler, lighter sequel" and "a noticeably slighter book," not as "deep" or as "true" as the "strikingly original" *Silence in the Snowy Fields* (1984, 186, 188). It lacks *Silence in the Snowy Fields*'s "sense of things 'obeying what is beneath them'" (186), as Bly had said in his poem "Night" (Bly, 1962, 55). Nelson says that he misses in *This Tree Will Be Here for a Thousand Years* Bly's tapping of "unconscious sources," the use of the journey motif, and the resonance of the Minnesota landscape that had been so pervasive in and important to *Silence in the Snowy Fields*.

Arguing that Bly's "weaknesses and strengths often lie close together," Nelson criticizes critics who, like Weinberger (1979), fail to notice complicities between *This Tree Will Be Here for a Thousand Years* and Bly's other work, both earlier and later. Nelson believes that *This Tree Will Be Here for a Thousand Years* contains clear signs of "developments . . . still to come" (188-89), and he takes to task critics who fail to separate the positive and negative elements in Bly's work and either oversimplify or distort it through their hostility to "his ends, means, or personality" (186). For Nelson, Bly's "extraordinary psychic and sensory richness" and his "intuitive moments" are the "principal reward of *This Tree Will Be Here for a Thousand Years*" (187). He considers the book a "sort of annex" to *Silence in the Snowy Fields*, perhaps most important finally (both to Bly's canon and to the criticism of his canon) for its suggestions of "developments" still to come (188, 189). Among these developments Nelson mentions Bly's growing awareness of his own mortality and the significance of his relationship with his father — as well as his relationship with "the Father" (193).

Looking most specifically at *Gott-natur*, the "new aspect" in Bly's work during the 1970s, Sugg considers *This Tree Will Be Here for a Thousand Years* in the larger context of Bly's obsession with "nature, human nature, and *Gott-natur*," "the divine instinctuality of nature's persistent energy" (1986, 104, 119). Bly is no longer either the "curious observer" he had been in *The Morning Glory* or the "passionate believer" he had become in *This Body Is Made of Camphor and Gopherwood* (1977), and the poems of *This Tree Will Be Here for a Thousand Years* emphasize, as the title clearly suggests, "survival and endurance" (113). Referring to the essay "Recognizing the Image as a Form of Intelligence" (1981a), in which Bly suggested that "when a poet creates a true image, he is gaining knowledge" and "bringing up into consciousness a connection that has been forgotten, perhaps for centuries" (21), Sugg argues that *This Tree Will Be Here for a Thousand Years* skillfully merges the "psychic weight" of Bly's personal life with the "eternal laws of the *Gott-natur*" and thereby affirms the relationship between "the individual and the eternal" (113-14). Bly's "thanatos instinct," Sugg thinks, dominates the first section of the book, the portion originally published as *Old Man Rubbing His Eyes*. The second section differs in tone and theme, and its poems contrast the differing "consciousnesses of nature and man" and treat their "shared consciousness" as they move "through despair to hope," with the concluding dozen poems emphasizing the "magnitude of nature" and the necessity that human consciousness "learn to locate itself within this larger context" (114, 117, 119).[2] At the end of *This Tree Will Be Here for a Thousand Years*, Sugg argues, Bly has turned to an admixture of "religious language and parable" to describe the "new state of mind" that *This Tree Will Be Here for a Thousand Years* introduces into his work at this point in his career (120).

Davis stresses the structural and thematic associations between *This Tree Will Be Here for a Thousand Years* and *Silence in the Snowy Fields*. Although both books represent a journey, the journey in *Silence in the Snowy Fields* is "outward, and chronological" while that of *This Tree Will Be Here for a Thousand Years* is "circular and cyclical" (1988, 33). These recent poems, however, are "deeper and darker" than the poems of *Silence in the Snowy Fields*. They describe the "energy circling downward" Bly had discussed in "The Two Presences" preface and also a "sense of things vanishing"; thus they suggest a "crucial turn toward the father and a growing sense of man's mortality" as opposed to the attraction for "mother figures and immortal nature" that is evident in *Silence in the Snowy Fields* (33-34). Taken together, these two books represent the "dominant mode of [Bly's] most representative work" to date and provide the "basis for much of Bly's later work" (39). Davis argues that the dichotomy between *This Tree Will Be Here for a Thousand Years* and *Silence in the Snowy Fields* anticipates the themes and modes of Bly's brace of books to come: *The Man in the Black Coat Turns* and *Loving a Woman in Two Worlds*. *This Tree Will Be Here for a Thousand Years*, Bly's "return to his beginnings" and his "book of renewal," represents "the return and beginning again" that many writers experience in mid-career. It is a book in which "loss is gain and emptiness suggests the presence of the fullness it has displaced" (35, 39). Therefore, as Davis says, *This Tree Will Be Here for a Thousand Years* describes the "process, already completed," that the poems of *Silence in the Snowy Fields* began — even if it is "a darker beginning," the book of a man who has "turned toward home and toward death" (34, 35).

[2]See *News of the Universe: Poems of Twofold Consciousness* (1980b), in which Bly refers to "call" poems, which, he says, describe "the call one form of consciousness makes to another" (35). Sugg calls *News of the Universe* "a virtual catalog of Bly's acknowledged influences" and "indispensible" as "Bly's own textbook on himself" (121).

6: The Poetry of Male Consciousness: *The Man in the Black Coat Turns*

AT THE BEGINNING OF THE 1980s, Bly's work took a new turn. Perhaps this was inevitable after the return and renewal evidenced by his work during the 1970s. Perhaps it was inevitable for reasons related more to his life than to the literature. Whatever the causes, the shift that began with *The Man in the Black Coat Turns* (1981) was immediately conspicuous and almost as quickly controversial from a critical point of view. As Davis points out, *The Man in the Black Coat Turns* is Bly's "symbolic turn toward home," the "self-referential elegy" that "many writers come to." As such, it describes and details the "end of the journey that *Silence in the Snowy Fields* had begun almost twenty years before." Still, it is "more than a simple return" and should most properly be seen not as "an end but [as] another new beginning." Furthermore, *The Man in the Black Coat Turns*, together with its companion volume, *Loving a Woman in Two Worlds* (1985), contains the most personal and private poems Bly has yet written. These two books therefore relate a great deal about Bly, man and poet, both where he has been and where he is going (1988, 133).

The poems in *The Man in the Black Coat Turns* are poems of "male consciousness," and Bly has had a lot to say about what he took this term to mean. In the introduction to the selections from *The Man in The Black Coat Turns* in his *Selected Poems* (1986) Bly said, "In this book I fished in male waters, which I experienced as deep and cold but containing and nourishing some secret and moving life down below" (142). Surely it is the case that the significant contrasts in the critical response to Bly's poetry in the 1980s can often be specifically linked to the differing positions various critics have taken with respect to Bly's statements and actions outside of his poetry. Since this is so conspicuously the case, a brief summary of Bly's views on male consciousness is almost inevitable.

The Man in the Black Coat Turns took Bly more than ten years to write (Bly, 1981), and he has said that he wanted the poems "to rise out of some darkness beneath us" (Bly, 1986). As early as 1971, he mentioned the emergence of a "spiritual inflation" that marked a new stage of father consciousness in his thinking and his work (1971). In the following years he often discussed his theories of father con-

sciousness or male consciousness in articles and interviews. In one of
the most important of these, in 1976, he described his father, who "had
to become a man too soon," "wearing a large black coat," "pursued by
grief and depression," but possessing a "gift for deep feeling," so that
other men "bobbed like corks around his silence" (205). Bly described
himself, growing up, as a "typical 'boy-god'"; but, he said, he learned
through his father's example that "the indignation of the solitary man
is the stone pin that connects this world to the next" (209, 217).[1]

In many instances and a wide variety of places Bly has considered
the implications of male consciousness on his thinking and for his po-
etry. In 1986, he discussed the "four seasons" of male development,
which "amount to four stages, four steps and four events": "bonding
with and separation from the mother," "bonding with and separation
from the father," finding "the male mother," and "the interior mar-
riage" with the "Invisible Czarina" of the Russian fairy tales (1986a,
42, 48). In his *Selected Poems* Bly said that these poems were "thoughts
that I have thought for years." "I aim in these poems," he said, to
"please the old sober and spontaneous ancestor males" (1986, 143,
144). In *Iron John: A Book About Men* (1990) Bly discussed the "deep
male" and the need to accept "the *nourishing* dark," to find the "dark
way" to the "Wild Man" by "taking the road of ashes," "learning to
shudder," and "moving from the mother's world to the father's
world" so that "our sacrifices" would be "appropriate" rather than
"unconscious, regressive, pointless, indiscriminate, self-destructive,
and massive" (1990, 6, 70, 79, 240).[2] In *The Rag and Bone Shop of the
Heart: Poems for Men* (1992) Bly spoke of "masculine sadness" as "a
holy thing" and the "growth of a man" as "a power that gradually ex-
pands downward" in such a way that men "are more alive" as they
grow older (97, 98).

Many of Bly's critics responded to *The Man in the Black Coat Turns*
in the context of male consciousness. A representative sampling of
these responses, which vary considerably, would include, on the one
hand, Richman, who notes that *The Man in the Black Coat* was heralded
as Bly's "long overdue reconciliation" with masculine consciousness

---

[1]For additional comments by Bly on this period of his life and work see
Siemering (1975/76), Thompson (1982, 1984), Wagenheim (1990), and
Appelbaum (1990).

[2]Bly's controversial *Iron John: A Book About Men* immediately became a best-
seller and remained on the New York Times best-seller list for more than a
year — most of that time at the top of the nonfiction list. (Several years
earlier, in 1987, Bly had published in embryo the basic theme and thesis of
Iron John in *The Pillow & The Key: Commentary on the Fairy Tale Iron John*.) For
a representative sampling of the critical responses to *Iron John*, see the
Appendix, "*Iron John: A Book About Men* and the Critics."

even though he feels the poems are only "vaguely 'about' masculinity" and that "little else had changed" in this book with respect to Bly's work (1986, 44); and, on the other hand, Davis, who stresses the importance of the male consciousness thesis in the context of the theme of the father-son relationship that is so important in *The Man in the Black Coat Turns* and in the context of Bly's buttressing the book with the work done by Marie-Louise von Franz and others in the area of masculine psychology (1988, 137, 145).

Throughout his career Bly had supported his theoretical speculations without regard for any rigidly logical, or even any specifically consistent pattern or application; each of the various disciplines he borrowed from he drew from in the widest possible ways and applied in whatever ways seemed most useful or necessary to him at any given time. In this phase of his career, he relied heavily on Marie-Louise von Franz's *The Feminine in Fairy Tales* (1976), *Shadow and Evil in Fairy Tales* (1980), and *Puer Aeternus* (1981); on James Hillman's *The Myth of Analysis: Three Essays in Archetypal Psychology* (1978), *Re-Visioning Psychology* (1978), and *The Dream and the Underworld* (1979); and on Erich Neumann's *The Great Mother: An Analysis of the Archetype* (1963), Joseph Campbell's *The Hero with a Thousand Faces* (1968), C. G. Jung's *The Spirit in Man, Art, and Literature* (1971) and *Four Archetypes* (1970), Jacob Boehme's *Dialogues on the Supersensual Life* (1901) and *Psychologia Vera* (1846), and the work of other thinkers — many of whom he had used and built upon earlier in his career as well. The most detailed tracing of these sources and influences throughout the course of Bly's career can be found in Howard (1969), Gitzen (1976), and Davis (1979-80, 1988, 1992).

When *The Man in the Black Coat Turns* was published in 1981 it was greeted with the same kind of ambivalent, if not quite as antithetical, responses from reviewers as those that had greeted *This Body Is Made of Camphor and Gopherwood* and *This Tree Will Be Here for a Thousand Years.*

These reviews of *The Man in the Black Coat Turns* ranged from an estimate that considers it "thoughtful" and thus more accessible than Bly's earlier work (Anonymous, 1981) to others that find it filled with powerful and "surprising" meditations more committed to their own "unfolding" than to any "end result" (Roffman, 1981) or filled with clichés and thereby evoking only "conditioned responses" (Anonymous, 1982), in which the "carefully chosen details" are too often "interrupted by silly interjections" or arbitrarily "broken off" (Jarman, 1982). One reviewer even calls it "a clear case of an established important poet larded by his own theories and specialties of style, turning them into fetishes" or "self-consciously trying to be the poet we expect him to be" and thus writing poems that "fit his theories" in an attempt to "prove them valid," with the end result that the poems mean "little" even though they have "the facade of Bly's earlier, better work" (Miller, 1983). Other critics responded to this "somber" book and to its poems with their "dark interiors" (Stitt, 1982) whose surfaces "crackle with energy and liveliness" (Stitt, 1992, 289), by labeling it a book "hauntingly" allusive and heavily suggestive, representing an impressive accomplishment in the "modern mainstream" (Stuewe, 1982) by a poet who had "never been more moving" (Jarman, 1982) — indeed, a powerful, impressive accomplishment, "easily [Bly's] richest, most complex book" (Stitt, 1982).

A suggestion of the animosity that this book evoked among reviewers can be seen in Miller's comment on Stitt's review: "Unfortunately, Bly's reputation is so formidable [that] it can cause a reviewer in *The New York Times Book Review* to call this collection Bly's 'richest, most complex book,' an absurd statement from my viewpoint" (1983).

Several of the reviews of *The Man in the Black Coat Turns* are particularly noteworthy. Perloff considers the "autobiographical" "concentration on fathers and sons" (which, she says, Bly had gotten from Theodore Roethke, one of his "central precursors," and from Robert Lowell, his "arch-enemy") and suggests that this autobiographical tendency represents a "swerve" toward the mode Bly had "always scorned" — indeed, even "dismissed as trivial and exhibitionistic" — as going counter to his earlier and stronger habit of writing a "poetics of immanent presence" (1982, 221). Therefore, she argues, there is a problem in reconciling the belief that poetry depends upon "the privileged moment when consciousness" enters the "realm of otherness" with "the linear story line of one's own life" (222). Bly's poetry in *The Man in the Black Coat Turns* is given over to "tendentious statement[s]," and it represents a sentimental falling off from his earlier poetry of images, as the *I* of *Silence in the Snowy Fields* becomes "pontifical" in *The Man in the Black Coat Turns* (224). In short, Bly has covered his tracks "all too successfully" (225) in many of these poems — such as "My Father's Wedding," in which the "Father becomes Norwegian deity becomes vegetation god becomes Christ becomes a 'massive masculine shadow.'" What these "mythic correspondences are meant to signify therefore remains murky" (225-26) and the poems are reduced to "phrase-making" and "the absence of meaning" (212). Perloff cites "Eleven O'Clock at Night" as one example of such "murkiness."

Wesling describes *The Man in the Black Coats Turns* in terms of the "theme of male grief" and the relationship between a son and the "father he will replace" as well as the "son who will replace him" (1981a, 447). (Bly dedicated *The Man in the Black Coat Turns* to his son

Noah Matthew.) This book, Wesling states, deals with "the great untouched subjects of fatherhood and replacement," and in it Bly is best considered as a "preacher or wisdom-writer" (448). This book, he goes on to say, contains some of the best poems Bly has ever written.

Always one of Bly's most conscientious critics and reviewers, Molesworth considers the "loose stylistic unity" of *The Man in the Black Coat Turns* and finds the poems "challenging," representative of Bly's "ethic," and founded on "the principle of growth." These poems (especially the prose poems, which Molesworth regards as Bly's best work) are, he argues, distinctive poems that subtly examine the intersections of "waking and archaic consciousness." In "Finding an Ant Mansion" in particular, he says, Bly's "spiritual allegorizing" is "most forceful" and focused. Nevertheless, Molesworth thinks, the poems in this book will "take some getting used to" even for Bly's "partisan readers" (1982, 283).

Finally, Reynolds in a review that takes into consideration many of the earlier reviews and points toward the more substantial criticism of *The Man in the Black Coat Turns* and Bly's work still to come, argues that even before the feminist movement had reached national visibility, Bly had been "advocating the female principle as a viable alternative to male-dominated consciousness" (1983, 439). In this sense Bly has been prophetic in anticipating the temper of the 1970s, though his readers would be disappointed were they to expect a "similar prophetic vision for the 1980's," since, if *The Man in the Black Coat Turns* is prophetic, "its prophecy lies in its poetics" (440). In the "meditative" and "death-ridden," even "violent," transitional poems of *The Man in the Black Coat Turns*, Bly, like the man in his title, may be a man turning toward "new vistas" or toward "his own death" (439, 440). The man in the black coat who turns "may be death who turns to wait for the poet." Consequently, although Bly "reaffirms his missionary stance," he "breaks no new ground" in this book. Therefore, Reynolds feels that what is to come next will be "crucial for Bly" (442).

Only a few significant critical articles have been published to date focusing specifically or definitively on *The Man in the Black Coat Turns*. Peters, stating that Bly's "techniques match up with his theories," thinks the book represents "an advance of impressive dimensions" over his previous work and "should prove [to be] one of the seminal works of the eighties" (1982, 305). He analyzes a number of poems in the book and finds in them a "koanlike quality" of "unresolved suggestiveness" and a "thrill" in the "proximity to Death." In the "father consciousness" poems Peters detects a merging of Bly's "own father- and sonhoods" in such a way that Bly "retrieves the specific from the universal" and redirects this motif to himself (311, 313).

Bly knows that *The Man in the Black Coat Turns* is both "another new beginning" and "the beginning of the end," as Davis says (1982a 237). In this book, which contains some of the most "authentic" poems Bly has written, he has opened the "door of the self" in a way he has never done before (238). Tracing Bly's work through a series of thinkers (Jacob Boehme, Nicolas Berdyaev, Sigmund Freud, C. G. Jung, Paul Tillich, and Martin Heidegger), Davis tracks his metaphor of darkness as "source," as "meaning deferred" and "developed around the metaphor of light," through Bly's earlier work and shows how it has been brought to climax in *The Man in the Black Coat Turns* in such a way that the "treasures of darkness prophesied" in *Silence in the Snowy Fields* and *The Light Around the Body* are "here, finally, fully fulfilled" (239-40). Just as in *News of the Universe: Poems of Twofold Consciousness* (1980), Bly's anthology that traces poetic history and attempts a "historical rediscovery of the poetic fathers" from his own point of view, so too in *The Man in the Black Coat Turns* Bly has attempted to rediscover his own "literal personal father(s)" (241).

The books on Bly develop many of the suggestions made by reviewers and other critics of *The Man in the Black Coat Turns*. Nelson, for instance, calls it "an extended meditation on the masculine soul" at the center of which is the "distinct and memorable figure of the poet's own father" (1984, 193). But other father figures are there too: the Father God, the Father Christ, and Odin the "All-father." These are mixed and merged in poems like "My Father's Wedding," "The Prodigal Son," "Crazy Carlson's Meadow," "The Grief of Men," and others. In Nelson's view, Bly's contemplation of fathers and sons, of the "male soul," and of the "grief of men" is "at the heart" of the book, as the "motif of sacrifice," strong throughout the work, increases toward the end of it, and comes to climax in "Kneeling Down to Look Into a Culvert," the final poem, which Nelson calls "a remarkable expression of a remarkable moment of consciousness" (218-19). Nelson finally sees *The Man in the Black Coat Turns* as "an affirmative book" in which Bly merges a "desire for healing and reconciliation" with an awareness of "griefs which do not heal" (230). Richman attacks Nelson as one of the "critics in Bly's thrall" who respond to this book "by relinquishing their critical powers." He charges that Nelson "discovers allusions, 'sexual metaphors,' 'symbols,' and coherent imagery everywhere in the Bly *oeuvre*" and says that "Nelson's ability to misconstrue Bly's poetry . . . is remarkable." He concludes, "For Bly and his critics, it is not enough for poetry to appeal to a primitive level of consciousness. It must be 'composed' by that consciousness too" (1986, 44-45).

For Sugg *The Man in the Black Coat Turns* presents Bly's "new subject," the "family of man," a family that by the end of the book has been redeemed through Bly's imagination in such a way that it is "neither unprepared for nor unjustified" (1986, 122-23). Bly's "psychic urge" to explore "man's identity" (most specifically in terms of the father-son dichotomy) is evidenced throughout the book even if this "archetypal figure/force" remains "unexplained and unpredictable." Bly's voice in these poems, Sugg feels, has taken on the "impersonality of someone who is trying to understand his life in terms of universal patterns." By the work's end Bly has made a "declaration" both about this book and about his canon to date. Like Thor on the Norse Doomsday, he would, in the words of Turville-Petre (1953), "step back dying, but not dismayed." In *The Man in the Black Coat Turns*, Bly has found a "new use" for poetry, a way to "enter into the stream of nature's energies" (125, 131, 141).

Davis argues that the "recovery of the shadow," which Bly described at length in *A Little Book on the Human Shadow* (1986), and the father-son relationship, which he detailed in his essay "Being a Lutheran Boy-God in Minnesota" (1976) and in his poems "Finding the Father" in *This Body Is Made of Camphor and Gopherwood*, and "The Grief of Men" and "My Father's Wedding 1924" in *The Man in the Black Coat Turns*, become the main foci of *The Man in the Black Coat Turns*. He notes that at the end of this book, "in a ritual that symbolized" a "sacrificial death as prelude to a new birth," Bly, "like the man in the black coat, fulfills all the implications of the final word of the book's title, and *turns*" (1988, 151). Thus, this book, Davis says, tells Bly's readers and critics "a good deal about him now" and a great deal about "where he has been and where he is going" (133). Therefore, *The Man in the Black Coat Turns* both brings Bly's early work to climax and anticipates his work to come.

Harris, describes *The Man in the Black Coat Turns* as Bly's personal "archives" (1992, 103). Less "solipsistic" and "visionary" than his earlier work, these poems document "a record of life in the daily world" and trace the "history of men in a man" (105-6, 117). In this sense *The Man in the Black Coat Turns* represents "a Bly we have not seen before." The central theme and focus of these poems, which Harris defines as the "neglect of the male," shifts, she says, "from subject to self to psychic inadequacy" through the course of Bly's "incorporative journeying" in the book (110, 112, 121). In a more recent piece, she calls *The Man in the Black Coat Turns* "a gorgeous volume" in which Bly "contends with the consciousness that he has" and makes manifest both the collective unconscious and the "personal consciousness within its participatory universe" (1992a, 172).

Thus, there was considerable critical agreement about the poems in *The Man in the Black Coat Turns*. They were, the consensus seemed to suggest, both backward-looking and forward-looking; in them Bly succinctly summarized a number of his most important themes in especially immediate, revealing, and rewarding ways; and in the final section of the book he drew together his dominant theme of the father-son relationship, especially in "The Grief of Men," which Davis (1992b, 274) called "clearly the climactic thesis piece for the whole book," as he completed his portrait of male consciousness.

7: The Poetry of Female Consciousness: *Loving a Woman in Two Worlds*

IF BLY HAD MADE A NEW BEGINNING with the poems in *The Man in the Black Coat Turns*, focused as they were on "male consciousness," he turned to the other side of the dichotomy with *Loving a Woman in Two Worlds* (1985), which focused on "female consciousness." Since they so specifically complement one another from a thematic point of view and complement Bly's social and political activities with women's and men's groups during the 1980s, these two books ought properly to be read and even criticized together. Taken together, they are Bly's most personal and private poems, and, partly because they are inseparably associated with his life outside his literary life, they have become his most controversial poems since *The Light Around the Body*. Nonetheless, for the most part, they have been treated individually by Bly's critics and reviewers, as they are here.

The other most conspicuous element of the critical response to *Loving a Woman in Two Worlds* is that these poems, when they have not been almost completely ignored, have been the least seriously analyzed and the most fiercely attacked of all of Bly's poems. This is the case even though they represent another stage in Bly's "corrective response to his own earlier sexism," as Lammon suggests (1991, 110). The attacks have come from virtually all quarters; they began early on and have not yet fully abated.

There are several other rather obvious reasons for the critical climate that surrounds, indeed seems almost to envelop, the poems of *Loving a Woman in Two Worlds*, Bly's most recent individual collection of new poems.[1] First, it was quickly followed by Bly's *Selected Poems* (1986), which, not surprisingly, tended to eclipse it as well as all of the earlier books Bly had published. (Even Bly himself "seemed to shy away almost apologetically" [Davis, 1992, 18] from the selection of poems from *Loving a Woman in Two Worlds* that he included in his *Selected Poems*. In his prefatory note to them in the latter collection he wrote, "The poems are still close to me, and I won't say much about them. . . . Love poems . . . can so easily go out of tune" [172].)

---

[1] *What Have I Ever Lost by Dying?* (1992) consists of prose poems, many of them reprinted from earlier collections, as discussed in chapter four.

Furthermore, as Davis has suggested, perhaps the poems in *Loving a Woman in Two Worlds* "took critics by surprise, confused them," or "even a bit embarrassed them" (1992, 12). Clearly, most critics were not prepared for the kind of overt love poems they encountered in *Loving a Woman in Two Worlds*, although they might have remembered that as long ago as in his essay "I Came Out of the Mother Naked" Bly had said, "Matriarchy thinking is intuitive and moves by associative leaps" (1975, 32).

For all of these reasons, the critical responses to *Loving a Woman in Two Worlds* have been, as Davis indicates, "slight, sketchy, unsystematic, and largely unsympathetic"; indeed, its major thrust suggests that the male-female consciousness explored in *The Man in the Black Coat Turns* and *Loving a Woman in Two Worlds* has "resulted in some of the weakest poems Bly has written" — though, since critics have had little time to consider the poems, their opinions may constitute only an "interim report" and be "far from definitive or final" (1992, 12).

Loving a Woman in Two Worlds received the fewest reviews of any of Bly's major books. One reviewer even concluded that it was "not a book meant for reviewers" (Brumer, 1985). The reviews were short, for the most part, and they were divided between essentially positive and largely negative responses to the book.

The positive responses find these "sparsely egocentric" love poems "neither radically confessional nor violent" in their imagery but uniting "intimacy with natural mystery" and "connecting eros to nature" (Emery, 1985) — poems that are "beautiful, strange, tender and powerful," indeed "*great* poems," even if some of them tend to be "a bit imperfect" or "a bit preachy" (Brumer, 1985). One of the problems with *Loving a Woman in Two Worlds*, according to Brumer, is "how not to feel like a voyeur" while reading the poems. He concludes, however, that readers come to feel "emotionally close" to the lovers in the poems rather than feeling as if they were "voyeuristically watching them through little poem-like windows."

Other reviewers, although some of them think that Bly himself is often "noisy, preposterous, impolite, and self-inflated," nevertheless appreciate the beauty, simplicity and "truth" of these poems "written in flat language without resonance" that yet still perfectly resonates with meaning — even if the meaning is "hardly in the words" but rather that the words frame a meaning which remains "unstated" (Hamill, 1987). Such reviewers are grateful for the "precise, evocative word pictures," the ways that Bly has made "grief mystical" and "sadness liberating" (Raksin, 1987), and the ways in which the poems are, finally, simply "beautiful" (Hamill, 1987). In Dacey's view, these "weighty" poems, "soaked with feeling" and "strengthened by their willingness to face the failure of love," represented the "culmination" of Bly's career to date; indeed, "Bly has apparently been waiting for years" to write *Loving a Woman in Two Worlds*, "not because it has been of secondary importance . . . but because he considered it too important to hurry" it (1986).

In one of the negative reviews — which are often based on exactly the same criteria that the positive responses are based on — Stuewe calls *Loving a Woman in Two Worlds* "all too often simply embarrassing" in its inability to describe "anything resembling deeply felt emotion," and therefore a book that can "only detract from Bly's already somewhat problematic reputation" (1985). The single most negative review was brief and anonymous. This reviewer charges that Bly, "up to his old business of invocation and subcutaneous persuasion" and using his "familiar themes and methods," falls flat or ends up with poems that appear to be "contrived" or "full of quaint echoes of Donne and Freud," and that this "forced strangeness" and these curious juxtapositions, with their "undertones of reverence or foreboding," are "comically inappropriate" and often little more than verbal or emotional clichés. The reviewer concludes, "I mean, this book stinks, folks. No kidding" (1986).

Chappell, balancing the positive and negative estimates of the other reviewers, argues that, even if Bly has become an "undiscountable element of contemporary poetic taste," any poet who "fashions an extreme individual style," as he has, may discover that he has "forged his own manacles" and that his poems may "melt together in a monochrome haze." Nonetheless, he says, it is one "asset of an extreme style" that "even its most customary mannerisms may result in a good poem." Chappell perhaps best summarizes the theme of most of the reviews when he says that, though this book "holds no surprises," it has "broken no promises," and finally, it stands as an important addition to a body of work that has "impressively persuaded a generation of poets and readers" (1985).

The reading, thinking, and writing that served as a background to Bly's poetry of male and female consciousness and thus to both *The Man in the Black Coat Turns* and *Loving a Woman in Two Worlds* had its genesis in the same sources that had earlier given Bly his psychological buttressing for *Sleepers Joining Hands*. This influence was traced to Jung and others by Bly's critics in the earlier stages of his career (see chapters three, five, and six). At this later date, however, there was a noticeable broadening of the basically Jungian influence, specifically to include the work of Erich Neumann, one of Jung's disciples. Following Jung, who said that the creative process had a "feminine quality," and that creative work "arose from unconscious depths" in the "realm of the Mothers" (1971, 103), Neumann points out that "matriarchal consciousness" is "not confined to women" but exists in men too as part of their "anima-consciousness," and that this is particularly true in creative people since "the creative is by its inherent nature related to matriarchal consciousness" (1973, 43, 58; also see Neumann, 1963 and 1969). Clearly, such a linkage between Neumann's notions of female consciousness and creativity was immediately attractive to Bly, and it was no more surprising that he used these ideas in his work than it was that his critics noticed them and began to analyze this work in terms of these ideas and influences.

In the earliest important essay to explore the general background of the Jungian tradition in Bly's poetry, Libby points out the dichotomy between male consciousness and female consciousness that is conspicuously evidenced in Bly's work and then aligns the separate sides of this dichotomy as it has been worked out in the poems along Jungian lines: masculine consciousness involves logic, efficiency, repression, and the "control of the natural world"; feminine consciousness includes intuition, creativity, and a "mystic acceptance of the world." Furthermore, since only women can be "biologically creative," men feel the "aesthetic urge to create" outside themselves — in poetry, for instance (1972, 85).

Libby traces these notions back through Bly's work to *Sleepers Joining Hands* and even earlier, arguing that, based on the evidence of his poems, Bly had seen "the mother coming up" through the psyche as early as 1970 (1972, 85). (Bly himself said in *Selected Poems* that he had begun "the poems that eventually became *Loving a Woman in Two Worlds*" in 1973, [172].) Davis (1992) suggests that it might be possible to go even further back, to one of Bly's earliest poems, "A Man Writes to a Part of Himself" (in *Silence in the Snowy Fields*), to find the source for the poems in *Loving a Woman in Two Worlds*.

It is interesting here to consider Bly's comments on "A Man Writes to a Part of Himself":

I lived [alone] for several years in various parts of New York City . . . in small dark rooms . . . longing for "the depths". . . . I saw the estrangement as a story: a man lives in a modern city, aware of a primitive woman bent over ground corn somewhere miles away, and though he is married to her, he has no living connection with her. (*Selected Poems*, 12)

This "story" became the poem "A Man Writes to a Part of Himself," which ends with these questions:

Which of us two then is the worse off?
And how did this separation come about?

Dacey says that "A Man Writes to a Part of Himself" "can be treated as a lens through which to view" Bly's work generally. He suggests that the predicament Bly describes in the poem is "as much cultural as personal" and that the speaker is a "representative citizen of the modern West" (1979). Harris argues that, although this poem "clearly asserts Jung's economy of a psyche with both masculine and feminine sides," the "scaffolding" of the poem remains "patriarchal"; thus Bly "remains at its authoritative center" (1989, 125). Kalaidjian explicitly links this early poem to Bly's poetry of female consciousness and says that it "typifies Bly's early blindness to the feminine vision he would [come to] celebrate," as he here "condescends to his anima," since the "poet's feminine other is primitive" and "mute" and remains a "silent 'other' on the margins of male identity" (1989, 137-38). Lammon, surveying the earlier responses to this poem, suggests that most readers seem to be "interested in the 'part' of the man who is a woman," but that "as Bly's journey brings him to where he needs to be," he realizes that the "other 'part,' the 'man,' is the one he overlooked"; he also realizes that any synthesis between this man and woman becomes the "next step in a new dialectic" between men and women, between the poetry of male consciousness and female consciousness (1991, 209-10).

In several separate essays Victoria Frenkel Harris deals both generally and specifically with the feminine and the "female consciousness" in Bly's work. She considers the significance of intuition in poetry in general, the use of the "incorporative consciousness" in one of Bly's early poems, and Bly's use of female consciousness in yet another poem (see Harris, 1981, 1981a, 1985). She argues that in the literature of an era defined by the collapse of the "bifurcation" between the masculine and feminine natures, it is possible to find "psychic integration," and the "nurturing" of the "woman within the man." This sense of female consciousness, she feels, is especially evident in a poem like Bly's "Walking Where the Plows Have Been Turning" (Bly, 1979, 49), in which the reader can "witness" the "mythic woman powerfully" rising "within a male" (Harris, 1981, 123-24). In another essay, she says, with respect to "With Pale Women in Maryland," "Suddenly, the poem turns into a woman" (1985, 55).

In a later essay Harris broadens, extends, and somewhat changes her argument as she considers specific questions of sexuality in Bly's work and states that, although his "desire to recuperate the fallen status of women is unquestionable," his "brand of feminism," by "valorizing intuition" through the use of the concepts of Jung and Neumann, conceals "remnants" of the very patriarchy he denounces. Therefore, when "an actual woman appears" in *Loving a Woman in Two Worlds* — as opposed to *Silence in the Snowy Fields*, in which "no woman" at all ever emerges and the "female omitted is she who has been historically oppressed" — she "often retains the position typifying patriarchal portraits of women" (as "the object for the subject, man") and is "trivialized" because she "never speaks herself." She remains "only an object," only "the other, whose sexual plurality is reduced to the gap, a home for his fetishized penis" (Harris, 1989, 120, 126-27).

Rehder, likewise, criticizes Bly's treatment of women in *Loving a Woman in Two Worlds*. Although he singles out for specific attention "Letter to Her" as "another example" of Bly's "evasion of self-analysis," calling it a poem that "runs out of honesty" and, after the "powerful" first stanza, ends in an "inconsequential" and "obscure set of images as self-justification," Rehder describes the "woman" in "all the poems" in this book as an "extremely shadowy figure" who almost never speaks, has "no behavior," and whose "body is mostly metaphors." She only exists, he argues, as a "pretext for the poet's emotions" (1992, 278).

Kalaidjian discusses Bly's "attempts to elide history through a feminist poetics based in [the] depth psychology" of Johan Bachofen, Carl Jung, and Erich Neumann and finds that Bly's feminist verse is "contaminated" by patriarchal elements that "oppress even as they seek to celebrate feminine experience" (1989, 135). This is because Bly, though "lamenting sexual division," ironically perpetuates it by lodging his "feminish critique within Bachofen's myth of mother right" and thereby falls prey to Bachofen's "Victorian representations of women." Even though Bly tries "to talk back to patriarchy" through his use of the "idiom of the deep image," he often succeeds in projecting "feminine Eros" only in "passive" images rather than the "empowering images of otherness" (137, 138). Thus he fails to "reflect critically on the sources of his depth psychology," and his recent work lacks "revisionary force" and simply "escalates" the "psychosexual conflict" that has been evident from the beginning of his career — in the long poem "Sleepers Joining Hands," for instance, and even in his essay "I Came Out of the Mother Naked" (in *Sleepers Joining Hands*), in which, according to Kalaidjian, Bly tries to "empower women's otherness," even though "its feminine argument" is "flawed" (139, 140, 141).

Kalaidjian points out that "Bly's nostalgia for a prepatriarchal *her-story*" actually distorts the "historical experience of real women" (135). He cites, among others, Adrienne Rich, one of the most celebrated poets of Bly's generation, who argues that the "feminine principle" remains "elusive and abstract" for writers like Bly and seems to have "little connection with the rising expectations and consciousness of actual women." Bly and others, Rich feels, "betrayed much of the time their unconscious patriarchal parochialism" (1977, 62-63).

Of the books published to date on Bly, only two treat *Loving a Woman in Two Worlds*. Davis associates the male consciousness poems of *The Man in the Black Coat Turns* with the female consciousness poems of *Loving a Woman in Two Worlds* by showing how Bly's revision of "Fifty Males Sitting Together" from the first book — which, in revised form, became the first poem in the second — ties these two consciousnesses, and thus these two books, together. Furthermore, he stresses the testing of the male consciousness of *The Man in the Black Coat Turns* by the female consciousness of *Loving a Woman in Two Worlds* as Bly, in "rough sequence," follows the course of a relationship between a man and a woman in *Loving a Woman in Two Worlds* and, at the same time, is seemingly trying to establish *Loving a Woman in Two Worlds* as a prelude to his *Selected Poems*, which was published the following year (1988, 153). Davis comes to the conclusion that *Loving a Woman in Two Worlds* is not as successful as it might have been, and he criticizes it for courting sentimentality and sometimes succumbing to it.

In hypothesizing about how love poems might go "out of tune" in the introductory comments to *Loving a Woman in Two Worlds* in *Selected Poems*, Bly said that if the poem "veers too far toward actual events," then its "eternal feeling" will be "lost in the static of our inadequacies," and that if "we confine the poem only to what we feel," then "the other person disappears" (172). Davis says that these "thematic considerations" are not what causes the love poems to go "out of tune" but rather the "poetic considerations," which Bly had not mentioned and which Davis does not specifically define (although it is clear that he means primarily the explicit matters of poetics). Finally, Davis finds *Loving a Woman in Two Worlds* to be representative of yet another transitional stage in Bly's career, one that has not yet been passed through and therefore cannot yet be properly or definitively evaluated.

In a chapter that recapitulates, somewhat extends, and, most significantly, tends to back away from some of her earlier assertions, Harris likewise sees *Loving a Woman in Two Worlds* as a companion piece to *The Man in the Black Coat Turns* and even argues that the two books, taken together, serve as "an impulse toward psychic completion" as Bly "finally confronts his shadow" in *The Man in the Black Coat Turns* and, then, in *Loving a Woman in Two Worlds*, "celebrates the love for which that confrontation freed him" (1992, 121, 126).

However, for Harris (echoing other critics), the "limitations of Jungianism" with respect to women complicates Bly's "incorporative efforts" in *Loving a Woman in Two Worlds*. Because his earlier poetry has stressed only the archetypically "'female' elements" within his masculine psyche, he has not encountered particularly complex problems; when he attempts to integrate the masculine and the feminine in an "interpersonal context," he encounters problems (121-22). These are especially evident in the "erotic" poems. Still, Harris believes, *Loving a Woman in Two Worlds* "celebrates the real woman Bly loves" and the "real love" that is made possible by "successful anima integration" — even though the "reduction of the female to body parts" in the erotic poems (thereby "accommodating her primarily to male sexuality") makes "such spiritual investment especially questionable" if not specifically "offensive" (129-31). Too often, Bly's "phallocentric perspective" leads to a situation in which the woman "is objectified, her sexuality marginalized, her body reduced to mere accommodation"; therefore, the "vision" of these poems can be "attainable" only by a "male subject" (135-36).

Throughout her commentary on *Loving a Woman in Two Worlds* Harris bolsters her position with references to other female writers and critics who, although they have not dealt specifically with Bly and his poetry, are nevertheless crucial to her argument and would be crucial to the further critical commentary on the female-consciousness focus and discussion in Bly's work. The most important of these sources for female-consciousness criticism referred to by Harris include Marie-Louise von Franz (*The Problem of Puer Aeternus*, 1970); Esther M. Harding (*Woman's Mysteries: Ancient and Modern*, 1971); Frieda Fordham (*An Introduction to Jung's Psychology*, 1975); Estella Lauter and Carol Schreier Rupprecht (*Feminist Archetypal Theory: Interdisciplinary Re-Visions of Jungian Thought*, 1985); Luce Irigaray (*Speculum de l'autre femme*, 1974, and *This Sex Which Is Not One*, 1985); Hélène Cixous ("The Laugh of Medusa," 1976); and Dianne Griffin Crowder ("Amazons and Mothers: Monique Wittig, Hélène Cixous and Theories of Women's Writing," 1983).

Harris concludes that while *Loving a Woman in Two Worlds* "delivers an actualized woman much of the time," the woman presented in the "sex poems" is "trivialized" and exists only as an object. Therefore, while Bly as done "more than any male poet in this century to privilege the feminine," his poems in this book are susceptible to the charge of the absence of discourse. When Bly turns from the poems that deal explicitly with sex, however, Harris argues that he achieves that sense of unity that has always been typical of his best poetry (136-37).

Bly's bifurcated, separated, but simultaneously integrated treatment of male and female consciousness in *The Man in the Black Coat Turns* and *Loving a Woman in Two Worlds* tended to divide his critics and cause some of them to change their minds about him, about his poetry, and about his work in general. What seemed to be needed next in Bly's career was some distancing that would allow the criticism to take his work into consideration over the long haul. Conveniently (as if he were already one step ahead of his critics), Bly's next book demanded such an overview.

8: The Poetry of an Uncompleted Canon: *Selected Poems*

BOOKS OF "COLLECTED" POEMS and collections of "selected" poems are very different books. Collected poems usually contain all of a writer's published poems. They are typically arranged either chronologically or in the order of the previous books. In either case, the poems left out of the published books, the unpublished and the uncollected poems (or at least a portion of them), are often added to fill out the canon. These collections usually appear after the poet's death or at least after the poet's canon is essentially complete. Such books are definitive.

Books of selected poems, on the other hand, especially when the poems are selected by the writer personally, are, by definition incomplete, and they are often unevenly balanced across the canon. Many poets select far fewer poems from the early books than ones from the later books, for instance. These books frequently include a selection of recent poems, never before published in a book, that both fill out the selection and provide the reader with the sense of something new. Such books insist that the writer is still alive, well, still writing.

Bly's *Selected Poems* (1986), a kind of "reader's guide" to his work (Stitt, 1992, 283), differs from all the seemingly well established norms for such collections. It is, as Davis says,

> unique in several ways. First, Bly took his title seriously. Considering the number of poems he had published in his career, this rather thin "selection" from his previous work might be thought of as extremely modest. Second, his book contained a large number of heavily revised or, indeed, totally rewritten poems. Third, it contained early, "new" poems — some never before published, others never before collected. Fourth, Bly rearranged the order of the poems from the previously published individual books for the sake of a new thematic unity in the *Selected* — even moving poems originally published in one book to a section largely devoted to another. Finally, Bly added short explanatory prose prefaces to each of the nine sections of the book, and appended two additional critical essays as "afterthoughts." In short, Bly's *Selected Poems* was as uncon-

ventional as, in some ways, each of this earlier individual books had been. (1992, 5-6)

Reviews of "collected" or "selected" books of poems also differ from reviews of other books of poems, and the reviews of Bly's *Selected Poems* were appreciably different from most reviews of such collections. This was nothing unexpected given the history of Bly's career and the unique nature of the *Selected Poems* itself. As Peseroff says, "This is not just an anthology of Mr. Bly's best work; its 11 new essays and its particular method of organization require a fresh look at the poet's achievement" (1986). Clearly, this is a "compact, convenient collection" that "succinctly" represents Bly in the "many individual phases of his work" (Davis, 1992b, 274).

Considering statements of this kind and the individual nature of the book, it is surprising that Bly's *Selected Poems* received far fewer reviews than some of his earlier books had and that there has not been, to date, any specific, detailed criticism devoted exclusively to the *Selected Poems* or to what Bly was apparently attempting to accomplish with it.

There are several ways to account for this lack of critical attention to Bly's *Selected Poems*. First, the unique nature of the book itself, so different from the stereotype for this kind of volume, might well have put critics off, at least initially; second, the book might have been considered essentially self-explanatory, thanks to Bly's own comments on the poems in the various sections, and therefore not in need of further commentary; third, the heavily revised poems and the rearranged text might have seemed to demand a much larger critical commitment than a simple review and thus some critics might well have been frightened away from it, or were not willing, for the sake of a review assignment, to attempt the larger critical task the book required or, indeed, demanded.

Other reasons for the lack of attention are also possible, of course. One would seem to have been that the critics had simply decided to pay Bly less attention than they had in the past. No doubt the most obvious reasons, however, were that Bly was moving very rapidly during these years, in many directions simultaneously and in several different genres, and he was attracting increasing attention as a "personality," outside of his role as a poet — as a "media guru," a men's-movement organizer, and a kind of cult figure with an increasingly larger following. It might therefore be argued that he deserved less attention as a poet because he had assumed so many other roles.

Bly's growing visibility as a popular personality was made evident by the media attention he was receiving and the coverage devoted to *Iron John: A Book About Men* (1990) in the popular press (see Appelo,

1991; Levine, 1991; and Morrow, 1991, for instance). *Iron John* appeared shortly after the *Selected Poems*; it received a great deal of attention, and Bly's work as a poet was in large part quickly overshadowed by his role in the men's movement. In some ways, then, the publication of *Iron John* eclipsed Bly's work as a poet, and this influenced the critical attention to the *Selected Poems* in particular.[1]

Finally, since no major new book of poems has yet appeared since *Selected Poems* (a very long silence for Bly), there has not been the critical demand for any more definitive appraisal of his earlier work in light of the new. (The only book-length criticism of Bly to appear late enough to have fully taken the *Selected Poems* into consideration, Harris, 1992, mentions it only in passing.)

Most of the reviews of the *Selected Poems* approach it, as Stitt does, as "a kind of reader's guide" to Bly's work (1986, 1024). Considering Bly's complete canon in terms of the *Selected Poems*, Stitt argues that, of the various ways of organizing such a body of work, Bly "reaches for the most indefinite locus of all," which he describes as "an area of the mind that is analogous to the deepest level of nature" (1022). Stitt begins his review by considering the ways in which books of poems — not just books of "selected" poems — ought to be "properly arranged"; he says that the "goal of coherence" is "certainly one that all poets must have in mind when putting together a book," whether or not they achieve such an end result (1021). Coherence is more difficult to achieve in a collection because the earlier books from which it is being made are "likely to be built on differing principles" of ordering than the collected or selected edition has been built on, and thus may well create "a sum rather different from the parts taken alone" (1021). Stitt asserts that Bly's book is "quite different from most such volumes" in that Bly has "pared his corpus down" to the "slim grouping" of the *Selected Poems*, which is "meant to indicate the major directions [he] sees his work taking" (1024). He defines Bly's two "major stylistic signatures" — made clear in the *Selected Poems* — as the use of metaphors "so strange that they can be called surrealistic" and an "odd," even "unintentionally funny," "surface" for poems that are finally "quite serious." Stitt concludes that Bly's commitment is always to "the dark, the primitive, the irrational" (1025-26).

Mitchell finds Bly's *Selected Poems* uninterested in history, which "destroys timelessness and the eternal" and, for all the specificity of his "placed" poems, finds that place is "almost incidental" in Bly's

---

[1]For a summary of the popular and critical response to *Iron John*, see the Appendix, "*Iron John: A Book About Men* and the Critics." Bly's most recent book, *The Rag and Bone Shop of the Heart* (1992), edited with James Hillman and Michael Meade, is an anthology subtitled *Poems for Men*.

work — it "is not that we see rural Minnesota" but "that we 'see' the eternal" 1988, 86, 89). For Mitchell, "Bly has become our principle tie to the residually primitive and mythic," and we may find in Bly, as Bly seems to find in his "snowy fields of rural Minnesota," a place to encounter the world anew" (87, 89). Even so, and even though Bly's "criticisms of the world are often just," simply because his poetry "avoids so much," it runs the risk of not seeing the world very well" or very "deeply." If Bly is not a prophet, at least, like Pound, he is within the "noble tradition" of "village explainers." Mitchell calls the *Selected Poems* "a disappointing book" because "we had been lulled into thinking over the years . . . that more had been accomplished." Still, Mitchell says, "American poetry was enlarged" by Bly, and it may be that Bly "is now poised to write the great work his work has always promised" (90, 91-92).

Other critics come to similarly ambivalent conclusions with respect to the *Selected Poems*, although most of them find more to admire in it than they do to criticize or condemn. Several clear exceptions are Rehder (1992) and Gioia (1987). Rehder says that the "elaborate, self-important prefaces" as well as Bly's "two 'after thoughts,'" insist so heavily on his "suffering and growth" because he is aware that the poems themselves "do not show very much development." It seems as if Bly hopes that his "autobiography" and his "awareness of his techniques" will somehow validate the poems (269). Gioia concedes that he likes the "sensibility" behind Bly's poems, "admires" "most of his basic values," and "delights" in Bly's "energy and irreverence." He wants Bly "to bring his poems to life — to dazzle, frighten and move" him, but he finds instead "page after page of predictable, edifying poetic exercises." This "decline into self-parody" makes the *Selected Poems*, for Gioia, "a major disappointment." He says that there is nothing subtle in Bly's "bid for major stature" since he has "unabashedly" organized his book to "demonstrate his own importance" and that this is made clear through his overt "chronicling" of "each and every" period of his career as his "compulsion to annotate his own work proceeds unchecked." Gioia says that Bly's organization of the book suggests that he "distrusts either his readers or his own work." Therefore, for Gioia, reading Bly's commentary "is like watching a ball game from the stands while listening to someone describe it on the radio. The announcer . . . seems to be describing an altogether different game, one much more exciting than the hum-drum contest down on the field." He concedes, however, that there are "a few breathtaking moments" in the book, as well as "many quiet revelations" — if only one did not have to "push through all the dullness and pretension to find them." He concludes that Bly's best poems

"make this volume worth the effort, but, unfortunately, it is an effort"
(222-23).

Most other critics do not go so far. Ardinger, for instance, argues
that Bly has "continually surprised us" with each new book and that
he has always had the ability to turn critics' heads in the directions he
wants them to go. He finds Bly's prefaces to the sections of the *Selected
Poems*, with his "candid remarks on his failed experiments" as well as
his elaboration of the expectations that have "fueled his most radical
intentions," to be "insightful and instructive" rather than "self-indul-
gent and superfluous." In short, he believes that the *Selected Poems*
provides readers with a "good vantage point" for surveying the whole
of Bly's work (1987).

Young treats Bly's career in terms of the "surrealism" that Bly and
others injected into the "bloodstream of American literature in a more
or less permanent way" in the 1960s. He suggests that the publication
of Bly's *Selected Poems* "helps remind us of that era, and its impor-
tance" and allows us to evaluate this surrealist influence on Bly's work
throughout his career. For Young, however, the verdict on these po-
ems is mixed because Bly's work is too often "forced" and of an
"uneven quality." "Bly's is a muse who often seems to be dragging his
poems into existence with a strained face and gritted teeth."
Nonetheless, Bly's invention of a "midwestern lyric" "replicates"
much of the life and landscape "from which it comes." And though
Young feels that many of Bly's achievements are "disappointing in the
aggregate" and that the poems for this collection "should have been
more rigorously selected," still, he says, one looks forward with antic-
ipation to the possibility of a resurgence of Bly's early "lyric strength"
in the next phase of his career (1987, 90-92, 93-94).

Melnyczuk calls Bly's *Selected Poems* "an idiosyncratic affair" — the
inevitable result of the poet's becoming "a guru, a bard of the people's
court, a hyper-vitaminized skald, a WASP shaman . . . a kind of
straight Allen Ginsberg." Even though Melnyczuk finds the "semi-
autobiographical prefaces" "variously illuminating and irritating" and
describes Bly as "capable of awesome banality," he concludes that the
book as a whole provides a clear chart of Bly's development toward
"integrity and wholeness" (1988, 167-68).

For Kakutani the *Selected Poems* reads like a "study in a poet's de-
velopment," a "sort of artistic autobiography" moving from the
"limpid haiku-like" poems of *Silence in the Snowy Fields*, through the
"noisy public pronouncements" on the Vietnam War in *The Light
Around the Body* and "The Teeth Mother Naked at Last," to the "more
pastoral mode" of *The Morning Glory* and *This Body Is Made of Camphor
and Gopherwood*. The introductions to the various sections of the book
seem "superfluous" or even "disturbing" to Kakutani because they

"impose themselves between the reader and the work"; indeed, because these introductions are too often either "sentimental" or "willfully naïve," they "tend to undermine" the rest of the book. Kakutani argues that the "vague, blissed-out 60's language" of the "mini-essay" introductions serves to point up "similar weaknesses" in the poems themselves. And, yet, for all the "blunt, chest-beating rhetoric" that assails "American hypocrisy and racism in clichéd sophomoric terms," there are poems here (those from *The Man in the Black Coat Turns* — "grounded in private, autobiographical details" and filled with "the ballast of felt emotion" — are cited specifically) in which Bly merges his "dark vision of world history" with his personal sense of "mortality," that reverberate "insistently in the reader's mind" (1986, 15).

Dacey sees Bly as an "American Norwegian Lutheran Buddhist pagan Sufi Jungian" saint, "regularly impressed by his own unworthiness," one who has "steadily played a sub-note of agony" and for whom literary form has become a "kind of religious device," a "prayer-wheel or rosary." Therefore, he says, Bly's career can be viewed as a "spiritual pilgrimage" and a "spiritual document," demanding "redemption" either by "looking out" or by "looking in" (1986, 13-14). Dacey discovers in the *Selected Poems* Bly's "confessionalism" in the old sense of the term and sees Bly as "the penitent" who "confesses" to a "father-(mother-?) confessor priest or spiritual guide"; or, perhaps more pertinently, he is "at once penitent *and* priest, the ailing who would heal himself and others." He regards the introductory essays to the various sections as "a mixed blessing." Even though "Bly is always brilliant as a prose writer," he is "not always reliable"; therefore these essays are sometimes "naked and moving and worth having" and at other times "embarrassments," filled with excesses" and "technico-mystical gobbledygook," that spread more "misinformation than information." Finally, however, the *Selected Poems* serves to "sharpen the outline of Bly's literary corpus, revealing how remarkably shaped, coherent, and self-referring it is" (1986, 13).

In one of the most definitively positive reviews of the *Selected Poems*, Peseroff calls the collection Bly's "record of the body's journey and the soul's quest" and also "a quest to find a voice to fit the poet and a prosody to fit the poem." She says that she knows of "no contemporary poet, except perhaps Allen Ginsberg, . . . who is so unafraid to write about joy," and she finds that the pleasure of reading these poems is that of discovering language, imagery, and themes that "recur, transformed," throughout Bly's work. Bly, "a public poet even in poems without overt political content," has never "believed that poetry makes nothing happen"; his poems "function like stained-glass windows in a cathedral" — they "direct us to wisdom and salvation" (1986, 2).

Bly's critics have all recognized that the *Selected Poems* is not the final word, that his poetic canon and the critical canon that has accompanied it for more than thirty years now are far from complete. Thus, the *Selected Poems*, which might have become "either a tombstone or a capstone" to Robert Bly's career, "appears to be a stepping stone" (Melnyczuk, 1988, 170); indeed, it is "a mellow ending to a good journey, one that is not over yet" (Peseroff, 1986, 2).

Conclusion

MORE THAN TWENTY YEARS AGO Bly was asked to comment on the significance of poetry — his own and poetry in general — for his life and for the world at large. He suggested that poetry and the "love of solitude" were "nearly indestructible" elements in human life, even though they lie "far down in the soil" of the subconscious mind. What poets do, he said, is attempt to bring "indestructible" longings up into conscious awareness and make them known in and to the world in their own time and for the world of the future, as an ongoing testimony to their time in human history (1970a). This is what great poets have always done, and their work and the criticism that surrounds it brings that work forward into the future and comes to represent that time in human history.

Robert Bly's career and the criticism of his life and work are far from over. He will continue to write; his critics will continue to respond to his work and to his life. Therefore, this history of the criticism Bly's work has received during these first thirty or so years of his career constitutes only the first stage, an early report, on what will surely prove to be one of the most extraordinary poetic careers in the twentieth century.

Appendix: *Iron John: A Book About Men and the Critics*

ALTHOUGH BLY'S *IRON JOHN: A Book About Men* (1990) does not literally fall within the specific focus of this book, which is devoted to the critical responses to Bly's poetry, it deserves attention here because, as Lense says, the poems in *Iron John* (both Bly's and the other poet's) "carry a great deal of the book's argument and emotional weight" since the premise of this book, like that of *Sleepers Joining Hands,* has its source in mythology and because *Iron John* is "developed by images rather than formal logic" (1993, 19). Furthermore, as Ross says, Bly's "career as a poet lends philosophical authority" to his position as the "paterfamilias" of the "emergent tribe of newly mature men" who make up the "men's movement" and who have made *Iron John* their almost sacred text (1992, 212).[1] And, of course, *Iron John* directly impinges on the criticism Bly's poetry has received, especially the poetry of *The Man in the Black Coat Turns* and *Loving a Woman in Two Worlds,* since these later books coincide thematically with Bly's activity in the "men's movement" (just as his earlier poetry coincided with his public opposition to the Vietnam War).

Iron John, like most of Bly's work, had a long gestation period, and it was preceded and followed by important essays and interviews, as well as TV appearances and videocassette recordings, in which Bly discussed portions of the book's text, the book in general, or various elements within it (see especially Bly, 1970c, 1976a, 1976b, 1979b, 1982, 1986a, 1987, 1989, 1990b, 1990c). Bly's critics and commentators responded — and continue to respond — to these issues (see especially Siemering, 1975, 1975/76; Daniels, LeMole and Goldman, 1978, 1978a; Bliss, 1978; Shakarchi, 1982; Bliss, 1987; Appelbaum, 1990; Moore and Gillette, 1990; Anonymous, 1992a; Kimmel, 1992; Seyfarth, 1992; Zipes, 1992; Kakutani, 1993; and Howard and Wagenheim, 1993).

Moore (1992), following his "intellectual mentor" Erik Erikson, argues that the "personal issues and problems" of "great cultural inno-

---

[1]Ross rightly says that even though Bly has "publicly distanced himself" from many of the "more theatrical excesses" of the men's movement, he is "recognized everywhere" as the "master-thinker" behind most of the men's movement activities (1992, 214).

vators" coincide with the "central problems of their age," and they act upon their age by dealing with their own problems and thus "help their culture address these issues on a wide scale." Moore believes that Bly's "contribution to our culture and our time . . . when evaluated by historians of the future," will prove to be such an example and that, primarily through *Iron John* and the men's-movement work he has done, Bly will come to be recognized as the catalyst for the "sweeping cultural revolution" that is imminent.

Almost immediately, *Iron John* received a surprisingly large popular following as well as a substantial critical response. Even though much of the latter was devoted primarily or completely to the social issues of the book, some of it inevitably spilled over into the criticism devoted to Bly as a poet (although many people who have read and written on *Iron John*, and even some who have attended Bly's lectures and seminars connected with the material of the book, seem largely unaware of his work as a poet — or have chosen to ignore it).

Since critics had a rather long time to prepare their responses to *Iron John* it is not surprising that these responses were rapid, numerous, and widely divergent. The reviews can be divided into those that appeared in popular magazines and treated *Iron John* primarily as a popular socially or psychologically oriented book, and those that appeared in journals or periodicals of a more scholarly nature and attempted to treat the book within the context of Bly's life's work, both as a commentator on the men's movement and as a poet and critic of literature.

The popular press was most impressed by the popularity of *Iron John*, as Ventura (1992) has shown. It was, as Levine says "the only self-exploration volume for men ever to reach bestseller status." Even so, as he notes, many people find Bly's ideas about men and masculinity "silly, if not downright dangerous" (1991). Several of Bly's reviewers clearly consider him dangerous. Garvey (1991) and Briggs (1992), for instance, go about as far as anyone does in stereotyping the way in which "so many" American men have "become a bunch of weenies." That, Garvey argues, is "why Bly and some of his buddies are getting rich by sending adult males out into the woods to get naked, dance around fires and howl at the moon."

Other reviewers in the popular magazines did little more than describe Bly — as a "scholarly cook" (Brumer, 1990); as "the rumpled 64-year-old lion of the men's movement" and therefore a "manful guru to the masses" or as a "self-help swami" (Appelo, 1991) who has the "annoying habit" of "quoting himself in the verse throes of manhood" (Warren, 1991); as the "high school valedictorian who went to hell" (a reference to Bly's celebrated solitary time spent in New York after he finished his academic training at Harvard and Iowa); as a "gifted poet, critic and shaman" who has "transformed his long struggle into a strange, mythicized American phenomenon" (Morrow, 1991); or as a man "speaking to men in search of soul" (Neafsey, 1991). Morrow raised the issue that it might be thought "odd" that Bly is not "more put off by the earnest vulgarity" of the men's movement and by his role in it.

Among the more serious treatments of *Iron John*, in which, as once critic says, Bly presents his position on "men's psychological developmental needs" as "exigent and transcultural" (Smith, 1991), are estimates by reviewers and critics who find Bly's book, and the "mythopoetic" (Gross, 1990) men's movement based on it, a "sweet and elaborate fantasy" or a "gentle frazzled text" (Eckhoff, 1991); "unworldly" in ways that could be "charming" or "batty" (Morrison, 1991); "instructive" and "ultimately exculpating" (Abrams, 1990); or "a sexy subject for ethnographers and sociologists" (Heller, 1993). Allen finds Bly's explication of the Iron John myth "deadly" as literary analysis and, as a "guide for living," "paralyzing" (1991). Johnston attacks the book as being "the story of Bly's own life" (1992). These and other "gender warfare" attacks raged in several periodicals, and Bly responded on several occasions to such attacks on him and on the men's movement and his involvement with it (see Bly, 1991, for instance).

Some critics caution that Bly's approach in *Iron John* seems to "encourage self-absorption" (Ziegenhals, 1992); that he tends to "overstate his views," a habit that is "part of the charm of poetry" but, in this context, "disconcerting if taken seriously" (Schmidt, 1991); and that he has perhaps given "insufficient attention" to the "violent, negative side" of the "passion and exuberance he celebrates" and therefore runs the risk of being misunderstood by men (and women) who have not read D. H. Lawrence and Erich Fromm (Johnson, 1992). Most critics, however, agree that Bly's "forays into the reconstruction of the male psyche" provide "reasonably convincing answers" and show a "sophisticated understanding of the dialectical nature of psychic reality," even if there are some "implied" shifts in "ontological and epistemological" perspectives involved (Csikszentmihalyi, 1990).

In short, *Iron John* was considered "important and timely" even if Bly's "prescriptions" for a "cure" are "difficult to assess"; at the same time, it was recognized that it was "easy to find fault" with a book that tries to accomplish "something as novel and difficult" (Csikszentmihalyi, 1990) as *Iron John* attempted.

There have been to date several substantial reviews, several important interviews, and several essays specifically devoted to *Iron John*. Tacey (1991) points out that Bly has established the social, historical, and psychological contexts for the "soft male" (a term that Bly coined or was the first to use) in his seminal 1982 interview "What Men Really Want" and that this interview, which has achieved almost cult status as a "fatherly rap over the knuckles," has had "considerable impact" in the "therapeutic (but not academic) community" (32-33). Tacey sees *Iron John*'s subject as "male initiation" or "rather the lack of male initiatory rituals in modern society." Though it holds "few intellectual surprises" and is "designed to satisfy a need . . . which, strangely enough, Bly himself has helped create," Tacey calls it a "major event" and a "book for the 'lost generation' of American men" (38, 40).

Hansen describes Bly's success with *Iron John* as the result of his "timely" combining in it the "two recurring subjects" that "dominate books that popularize psychological ideas": the application of the Freudian belief that many adults are not "whole or healed" because they have "not yet come to terms with some traumatic childhood experience, often familial," and the "Jungian concept of archetypes" that constitutes the "collective unconscious." Since *Iron John* explores "both of these currently fashionable subjects," it is not surprising that it is popular, even if "too often" Bly's description of the "eight-stage initiatory path" is "hard to make simple sense of." Therefore, Hansen feels, the book is "provocative" and "challenging" although it is also "repetitious" and "circuitous" and frequently suffers from the "directionless quality of good conversation (which no doubt much of it was and was intended to be seen as) with a thoughtful, enthusiastic person" (1992, 415, 417, 418).

Finally, Solotaroff argues that the men's movement (which he says derived from "A.A., feminism, New Age religion and therapy, environmentalism and the culture and charisma of Robert Bly"), which has put *Iron John* "at the top of the charts," has done so because, "for all of its discursiveness and highhandedness," Bly has managed in it, along with the "encyclopedic command of the great heuristic myths, legends and folklore that understand us," as well as the "learning he has acquired in the archeology and anthropology of the imagination," to combine "therapy" with "clarity" and to fashion a "deeply based counsel of self-empowerment and change" that manages "to hit paydirt about every third page" (1991, 270, 273, 274).

It must be remembered that the impetus for *Iron John* was Bly's interview with Keith Thompson (Bly, 1982) and that the first chapter, "The Pillow and the Key," was a rewriting of this interview (see Bly, 1990a, xi). Bly has also discussed *Iron John* in several recent interviews. Wagenheim (1990), who describes Bly as "one part mad professor, one part guidance counselor, one part wide-eyed schoolboy," discusses with Bly the background to his work with men's groups that led him to write *Iron John*, and Bly provides an extremely useful short sum-

mary of the book in this interview written on the verge of *Iron John's*
publication (see Bly, 1990d).

As the recent interviews indicate, the men's movement and *Iron
John* were not adjuncts to the woman's movement (as some had be-
lieved, especially because of Bly's long involvement with women's
groups before he turned his attention to working with men's groups),
and neither was *Iron John* a "backlash" against the woman's move-
ment, as Faludi (1991) and others were to charge. In his interview with
Myers (1992) Bly said that *Iron John* was his attempt to find "fairy sto-
ries that would be helpful for men" and that the story of Iron John,
which he said was "older than the Indian Vedas," "maps one of the
routes that can be taken from the position of being a boy to being an
adult man."[2] Myers describes *Iron John* as a book in which Bly has
"answered the call of the wild, and the grief, from within" (408, 409-
10). In another recent interview (see Udovitch, 1992) Bly indicated that
he might write another book, with more stories, "some with women
who are extremely independent." He also conceded that he had
thought a lot about his writing about men in the past several years
and that *Iron John* "would be different if I wrote it now" (36).

These reviews and interviews have been followed up by several
more substantial pieces, and others, no doubt, are forthcoming. The
several essays published to date are either clearly for Bly or against
him, or they are cautionary analyses in the form of recapitulations,
careful to avoid either extreme. Kuusisto calls *Iron John* a "devotional
book" or "a reverie" in which "medieval and Romantic images rever-
berate." These images aim to "discover charged heroic archetypes"
but fall into "page after page of Masonic prose" because Bly fails to
"probe the etiology" of the "Jungian imagery" he makes use of (1991,
79, 84-85, 86). Galin calls *Iron John* "a brilliant, compact, lyrical poem"
that "asks males to join hands with their ancestors and found a new
life"; it is, he says, a book that "changed the direction of my life"
(1992, 213, 214). Weissman writes that, "as a woman and an aca-
demic," she has been "overwhelmed with joy" over the "amazing suc-
cess" of *Iron John* which she calls an "articulation of truths" that have
been "denied" by much of the contemporary world. Therefore, she
hopes that women are reading *Iron John* and will discover, as she has,

---

[2]In this sense *Iron John* paved the way for other books on men and the men's
movement, as well as books on women and the women's movement.
Perhaps the best example of a women's movement book, one as popular as
Bly's *Iron John*, is Clarissa Pinkola Estés's *Women Who Run with the Wolves:
Myths and Stories of the Wild Woman Archetype* (1992). Kakutani (1993) argues
that *Iron John* has "indirectly begotten" both *Women Who Run with the Wolves*
and Marianne Williamson's *A Woman's Worth* (1993).

that Bly could be "a mentor, a male mother, for women as well as for men" (1992, 239, 241, 243).

Finally, True finds *Iron John* "a tired book" filled with "windy, abstract prose"; "disconnected and arbitrary meanderings" on a "myth that could mean just about anything"; and "reflections that clarify nothing" because Bly talks "nonsense much of the time." True says that, after this diversion of direction, he hopes that Bly will "return to his proper work" as poet and critic (1992, 238).

Since that is precisely where this book found Robert Bly in the first place, it seems appropriate enough, here at the end of it, to leave him there again.

Bibliography

All works are cited parenthetically in the text by author or editor and date.

Works by Robert Bly:

1958. "Five Decades of Modern American Poetry." *The Fifties* 1: 36-39.

1959. "On English and American Poetry." *The Fifties* 2: 45-47.

1959a. [Crunk.] "The Work of Donald Hall." *The Fifties* 3: 32-46.

1959b. [Crunk.] "The Work of Robert Creeley." *The Fifties* 2: 10-21.

1960. "On Current Poetry in America." *The Sixties* 4: 28-29.

1960a. [Crunk.] "The Work of W. S. Merwin." *The Sixties* 4: 32-43.

1961. "Poetry in an Age of Expansion." *Nation* (22 April): 350-54.

1961a. "Some Notes on French Poetry." *The Sixties* 5: 66-70.

1962. *Silence in the Snowy Fields.* Middletown, Conn.: Wesleyan University Press.

1962a. "Prose vs Poetry." *Choice* 2: 65-80.

1962b. With James Wright and William Duffy. *The Lion's Tail and Eyes: Poems Written Out of Laziness and Silence.* Madison, Minn.: The Sixties Press.

1962c. "On the Necessary Aestheticism of Modern Poetry." *The Sixties* 6: 22-24.

1963. "A Wrong Turning in American Poetry." *Choice* 3: 33-47.

1966. *A Poetry Reading Against the Vietnam War.* Madison, Minn.: The Sixties Press.

1966a. "The Dead World and the Live World." *The Sixties* 8: 2-7.

1966b. [Crunk.] "The Work of James Wright." *The Sixties* 8: 52-78.

1966c. "Concerning the Little Magazines: Something Like a Symposium." *Carleton Miscellany* 7: 20-22.

1966d. *The Sea and the Honeycomb*. Madison, Minn.: The Sixties Press.

1967. *The Light Around the Body*. New York: Harper & Row.

1967a. "On Political Poetry." *Nation* (24 April): 522-24.

1967b. "Leaping Up into Political Poetry." *London Magazine* 7: 82-87.

1967c. "The First Ten Issues of *Kayak*." *Kayak* 12: 45-49.

1967d. "Looking for Dragon Smoke." *Stand* 9(1): 10-12.

1968. "Acceptance of the National Book Award for Poetry, March 6, 1968." *Tennessee Poetry Journal* 2: 14-15.

1969. "Praise to the Opposites." *TransPacific* 1: 4-5.

1969a. *The Morning Glory: Another Thing That Will Never Be My Friend*. San Francisco, Calif.: Kayak Books.

1970. (Editor.) *Forty Poems Touching on Recent American History*. Boston: Beacon Press.

1970a. "Crossing Roads." *Prairie Schooner* 44(2): 146.

1970b. "A Conversation with Robert Bly." *Harvard Advocate* 103: 4-8.

1970c. "The Masculine Versus the Feminine in Poetry: An Interview with William Heyen and Gregory Fitz Gerald." [Videocassette recording.] Brockport, New York.

1970d. *The Teeth Mother Naked at Last*. San Francisco, Calif.: City Light Books.

1970e. *The Morning Glory: Another Thing That Will Never Be My Friend*. Second, revised and enlarged edition. San Francisco, Calif.: City Lights Books.

1971. "Symposium: What's New in American and Canadian Poetry." *New* 15: 17-20.

1972. "American Poetry: On the Way to the Hermetic." *Books Abroad* 46: 17-24.

1972a. "The Three Brains." *The Seventies* 1: 61-69.

1972b. "Looking for Dragon Smoke." *The Seventies* 1: 3-8.

1973. *Sleepers Joining Hands.* New York: Harper & Row.

1973a. "Developing the Underneath." *American Poetry Review* 2(6): 44-45.

1973b. "The War Between Memory and Imagination." *American Poetry Review* 2(5): 49-50.

1973c. *Jumping Out of Bed.* Barre, Mass.: Barre Publishers.

1974. *Point Reyes Poems.* Half Moon Bay, Calif.: Mundra.

1975. *Leaping Poetry: An Idea with Poems and Translations.* Boston: Beacon Press.

1975a. *Old Man Rubbing His Eyes.* Greensboro, N.C.: Unicorn Press.

1975b. *The Morning Glory.* New York: Harper & Row.

1976. "Being a Lutheran Boy-God in Minnesota." In *Growing Up in Minnesota: Ten Writers Remember Their Childhoods,* edited by Chester G. Anderson. Minneapolis: University of Minnesota Press.

1976a. "Praising Consciousness: Male and Female." *Ten Points: A Magazine of the Arts* (Summer): 11-15.

1976b. "Conversation with Robert Bly." [Interview with Kevin Power.] *Texas Quarterly* 19(3): 80-94.

1977. "What the Prose Poem Carries with It." *American Poetry Review* 6(3): 44-45.

1977a. *This Body Is Made of Camphor and Gopherwood.* New York: Harper & Row.

1978. "Where Have All the Critics Gone." *Nation* (22 April): 456-59.

1979. *This Tree Will Be Here for a Thousand Years.* New York: Harper & Row. (New, revised edition, 1992.)

1979a. "The Two Presences." In *This Tree Will Be Here for a Thousand Years.* New York: Harper & Row.

1979b. "Poet at Large: A Conversation with Robert Bly." WHET-TV New York (19 February): Educational Broadcasting Corporation.

1980. *Talking All Morning.* Ann Arbor: University of Michigan Press.

1980a. "Two Stages of an Artist's Life." *Georgia Review* 34(1): 105-9.

1980b. (Editor.) *News of the Universe: Poems of Twofold Consciousness.* San Francisco: Sierra Club Books.

1980c. "A Meditation on a Poem by Goethe." In *News of the Universe* 280-85.

1980d. "A Meditation on a Poem by Yeats." In *News of the Universe* 286-93.

1981. *The Man in the Black Coat Turns.* New York: Dial Press.

1981a. "Recognizing the Image as a Form of Intelligence." *Field* 24: 17-27.

1981/82. "Response to Frederick Turner." *Missouri Review* 5(2): 189-91.

1982. "What Men Really Want." [An Interview with Robert Bly.] *New Age Journal* (May): 30-37, 50-51.

1983. *The Eight Stages of Translation.* Boston: Rowan Tree Press.

1984. "In Search of an American Muse." *New York Times Book Review* (22 January): 1, 29.

1985. *Loving a Woman in Two Worlds.* New York: Dial Press.

1985a. "The Mind Playing." In *Singular Voices: American Poetry Today,* edited by Stephen Berg. New York: Avon Books.

1986. *Selected Poems.* New York: Harper & Row.

1986a. "Men's Initiation Rites." *Utne Reader* (April/May): 42-49.

1986b. *A Little Book on the Human Shadow*. Edited by William Booth. Memphis: Raccoon Books.

1986c. "Whitman's Line as a Public Form." In *Selected Poems*: 194-98.

1986d. "The Prose Poem as an Evolving Form." In *Selected Poems*: 199-204.

1987. *The Pillow & the Key: Commentary on the Fairy Tale Iron John*. St. Paul: Minn.: Ally Press.

1989. "Connecting with the Wild Man Inside All Males." [Interview with Keith Thompson.] *Utne Reader* (November-December): 58.

1990. *American Poetry: Wildness and Domesticity*. New York: Harper & Row.

1990a. *Iron John: A Book About Men*. Reading, Mass.: Addison-Wesley.

1990b. "Father and Son," In *Mother Father*, edited by Harry A. Wilmer. Wilmette, Ill.: Chiron Publications.

1990c. "A Gathering of Men with Bill Moyers and Robert Bly." (8 January) New York: Public Affairs Television.

1990d. "Stalking the Wild Man." *New Age Journal* (October): 43, 45.

1990e. *Ten Poems of Francis Ponge Translated by Robert Bly and Ten Poems of Robert Bly Inspired by the Poems of Francis Ponge*. Riverview, New Brunswick: Owl's Head Press.

1991. "Fantasies of Gender Violence." [A Letter.] *New York Times Book Review* (22 December): 4.

1992a. (Editor, with James Hillman and Michael Meade.) *The Rag and Bone Shop of the Heart: Poems for Men*. New York: HarperCollins.

1992b. *What Have I Ever Lost by Dying?* New York: HarperCollins.

Critical Works:

Boehme, Jacob. 1846. *Psychologia Vera, Sämmtlicke Werke,* Vol. 6. Edited by K. W. Schiebler. Leipzig: A. Barth.

_____. 1901. *Dialogues on the Supersensual Life.* Edited by Bernard Holland. London: Methuen.

MacLean, Paul. 1949. "Psychosomatic Disease and the 'Visceral Brain.'" *Psychosomatic Medicine* 2: 338-53.

Turville-Petre, E. O. G. 1953. *Origins of Icelandic Literature.* Oxford: Clarendon Press.

Frye, Northrop. 1957. *Anatomy of Criticism: Four Essays.* Princeton: Princeton University Press.

MacLean, Paul. 1958. "Contrasting Functions of Limbic and Neocortical Systems of the Brain and Their Relevance to Psychophysiological Aspects of Medicine." *American Journal of Medicine* 25(4): 611-26.

Anonymous. 1962. [Review of *Silence in the Snowy Fields.*] *The Booklist* (1 December): 274.

Clunk. 1962. [Review of *Silence in the Snowy Fields.*] *Burning Deck* 1: 58.

Hall, Donald, editor. 1962. *Contemporary American Poetry.* Baltimore: Penguin.

MacLean, Paul. 1962. "New Findings Relevant to the Evolution of Psychosexual Functions of the Brain." *Journal of Nervous and Mental Disease* 135(4): 289.

Anonymous. 1963/64. [Review of *Silence in the Snowy Fields.*] *Beloit Poetry Journal* 14: 39

Brooks, Cleanth. 1963. "Poetry Since 'The Waste Land.'" *Southern Review,* N.S. 1(3): 487-500.

Colombo, John Robert. 1963. "Poetry Chronicle." [Review of *Silence in the Snowy Fields.*] *Tamarack Review* 26: 86-95.

Derleth, August. 1963. "Books of the Times." [Review of *Silence in the Snowy Fields*.] *The Capital Times* (17 January): 20.

Fowlie, Wallace. 1963. "Not Bards So Much as Catalyzers." [Review of *Silence in the Snowy Fields*.] *New York Times Book Review* (12 May): 36.

Gunn, Thom. 1963. "Poems and Books of Poems." [Review of *Silence in the Snowy Fields*.] *Yale Review* 53: 142.

Hughes, D. J. 1963. "The Demands of Poetry." [Review of *Silence in the Snowy Fields*.] *Nation* (5 January): 16-18.

Jerome, Judson. 1963. "A Poetry Chronicle — Part I." [Review of *Silence in the Snowy Fields*.] *Antioch Review* 23(1): 109-24.

Jones, Le Roi. 1963. "The Colonial School of Melican Poetry (or, 'Aw, man, I read those poems before. . .')." *Kulchur* 10: 83-84.

Kelly, Robert. 1963. [Interview.] In *The Sullen Art: Interviews with Modern American Poets*, edited by David Ossman. New York: Corinth Books.

Mills, Ralph J., Jr. 1963. "Four Voices in Recent American Poetry." [Review of *Silence in the Snowy Fields*.] *Christian Scholar* 46(4): 324-45.

Neumann, Erich. 1963. *The Great Mother: An Analysis of the Archetype*. Translated by Ralph Manheim. Princeton: Princeton University Press.

Nordell, Roderick. 1963. "From the Bookshelf: A Poet in Minnesota." [Review of *Silence in the Snowy Fields*.] *Christian Science Monitor* (23 January): 9.

Rothenberg, Jerome. 1963. [Interview.] In *The Sullen Art: Interviews with Modern American Poets*, edited by David Ossman. New York: Corinth Books.

Simpson, Louis. 1963. "Poetry Chronicle." [Review of *Silence in the Snowy Fields*.] *Hudson Review* 16(1): 130-40.

Sorrentino, Gilbert. 1963. [Review of *The Lion's Tail and Eyes: Poems Written Out of Laziness and Silence*.] *Kulchur* 10: 84-86.

Stepanchev, Stephen. 1963. "Chorus of Versemakers: A Mid-1963 Medley." [Review of *Silence in the Snowy Fields*.] *New York Herald Tribune Books* (11 August): 7.

Stitt, Peter. 1963. "Robert Bly's World of True Images." Minnesota *Daily,*
  "Ivory Tower." (8 April): 29, 47.

Eshleman, Clayton. 1964. [Review of *Twenty Poems of César Vallejo.*] *Kulchur*
  14: 88-92.

Locke, Duane. 1964. "New Directions in Poetry." *dust* 1: 68-69.

MacLean, Paul. 1964. "Man and His Animal Brains." *Modern Medicine* (2
  March): 95-106.

Guest, Barbara. 1965. "Shared Landscapes." [Review of *Silence in the Snowy
  Fields.*] *Chelsea* 16: 150-52.

Mills, Ralph J., Jr. 1965. *Contemporary American Poetry.* New York: Random
  House.

Stepanchev, Stephen. 1965. *American Poetry Since 1945.* New York: Harper &
  Row.

Lindenau, Judith. 1966. [Review of *A Poetry Reading Against the Vietnam
  War.*] *South Dakota Review* 4(4): 89.

Zweig, Paul. 1966. "The American Outsider." *Nation* (14 November): 517-19.

Anonymous. 1967. "Chained to the Parish Pump." [Review of *Silence in the
  Snowy Fields.*] *Times Literary Supplement* (16 March): 220.

_____. 1967a. [Review of *The Sea and the Honeycomb.*] *El Corno Emplumado* 21:
  111.

Clayre, Alasdair. 1967. "Recent Verse." [Review of *The Sea and the
  Honeycomb.*] *Encounter* 29: 78.

Hamilton, Ian. 1967. "On the Rhythmic Run." [Review of *Silence in the Snowy
  Fields.*] *Observer* (20 March): 23.

M. R. 1967. [Review of *A Poetry Reading Against the Vietnam War.*] *El Corno
  Emplumado* (23 July): 149-50.

Rexroth, Kenneth. 1967/68. "The Poet as Responsible." [Review of *The Light
  Around the Body* and *A Poetry Reading Against the Vietnam War.*]
  Northwest Review 9(2): 116-18.

Simpson, Louis. 1967. "Dead Horses and Live Issues." *Nation* (24 April): 521.

Wheat, Allen. 1967. "Solitude and Awareness: The World of Robert Bly." Minnesota *Daily*, "Irovy Tower." (October): 19-23, 44.

Anonymous. 1968. "Special Pleading." [Review of *The Light Around the Body*.] *Times Literary Supplement* (15 August): 867.

Benedikt, Michael. 1968. "The Shapes of Nature." *Poetry* 113: 211-12.

Bland, Peter. 1968. [Review of *The Light Around the Body*.] *London Magazine* 8: 95-97.

Brownjohn, Alan. 1968. "Pre-Beat." *New Statesman* (2 August): 146.

Burns, Gerald. 1968. "U. S. Poetry 1967 — The Books That Matter." *Southwest Review* 53: 103.

Campbell, Joseph. 1968. *The Hero with a Thousand Faces*. Princeton: Princeton University Press.

Carruth, Hayden. 1968. "Comment." [Review of *The Light Around the Body*.] *Poetry* 112(6): 418-27.

Goldman, Michael. 1968. "Joyful in the Dark." [Review of *The Light Around the Body*.] *New York Times Book Review* (18 February): 10, 12.

Hamilton, Ian. 1968. "Public Gestures, Private Poems." [Review of *The Light Around the Body*.] *Observer* (30 June): 24.

Koestler, Arthur. 1968. *The Ghost in the Machine*. New York: Macmillan.

Leibowitz, Herbert. 1968. "Questions of Reality." [Review of *The Light Around the Body*.] *Hudson Review* 21(3): 553-57.

Mazzocco, Robert. 1968. "Jeremiads at Half-Mast." [Review of *The Light Around the Body*.] *New York Review of Books* (10 June): 22-25.

Simpson, Louis. 1968. "New Books of Poems." [Review of *The Light Around the Body*.] *Harper's* (August): 74-75.

Smith. 1968. "The Strange World of Robert Bly." *The Smith* 8: 184-85.

Symons, Julian. 1968. "New Poetry." [Review of *The Light Around the Body*.] *Punch* (25 July): 136.

Taylor, W. E. 1968. "The Chief." *Poetry Florida And* 1: 12-16.

von Bertalanffy, Ludwig. 1968. *General Systems Theory: Foundations, Development, Applications*. New York: Braziller.

Zinnes, Harriet. 1968. "Two Languages." [Review of *The Light Around the Body*.] *Prairie Schooner* 42(2): 176-78.

Zweig, Paul. 1968. "A Sadness for America." [Review of *The Light Around the Body*.] *Nation* (25 March): 418-20.

Fair, Charles M. 1969. *The Dying Self*. Middletown, Conn.: Wesleyan University Press.

Heyen, William. 1969. "Inward to the World: The Poetry of Robert Bly." *The Far Point* 3: 42-50.

Howard, Richard. 1969. *Alone With America: Essays on the Art of Poetry in the United States Since 1950*. New York: Atheneum.

Matthews, William. 1969. "Thinking About Robert Bly." *Tennessee Poetry Journal* 2(2): 49-57.

Neumann, Erich. 1969. *Art and the Creative Unconscious*. Translated by Ralph Manheim. Princeton: Princeton University Press.

Gullans, Charles. 1970. "Poetry and Subject Matter, From Hart Crane to Turner Cassity." *Southern Review* N.S. 6: 503-5.

Jung, C. G. 1970. *Four Archetypes*. Translated by R. F. C. Hull. *Collected Works*, Vol. 9, Part 1. Princeton: Princeton University Press.

Piccione, Anthony. 1970. "Robert Bly and the Deep Image." Ph.D. dissertation, Ohio University.

Eshleman, Clayton. 1971/72. "In Defense of Poetry." *Review* 4/5: 39-47.

Frye, Northrop. 1971. *The Critical Path: An Essay on the Social Context of Literary Criticism*. Bloomington: Indiana University Press.

Gitlin, Todd. 1971. "The Return of Political Poetry." *Commonweal* (23 July): 377.

Harding, Esther M. 1971. *Woman's Mysteries: Ancient and Modern.* New York: Putnam.

Heffernan, Michael. 1971. "Brief Reviews." [Review of *The Teeth Mother Naked at Last.*] *Midwest Quarterly* 12: 355-56.

Jung, C. G. 1971. *The Spirit in Man, Art, and Literature.* Translated by R. F. C. Hull. *Collected Works,* Vol. 15. Princeton: Princeton University Press.

Katz, Bill. 1971. "The Book Review." [Review of *The Teeth Mother Naked at Last.*] *Library Journal* (15 February): 641.

M. D. 1971. "Bookmarks." [Review of *The Teeth Mother Naked at Last.*] *Prairie Schooner* 45(1): 92-93.

Naiden, James. 1971. "Vietnam Everyone's Fault? Poetry Protesting War 'Crashing Bore'." [Review of *The Teeth Mother Naked at Last.*] *Minneapolis Star* (30 March): 1B.

Anonymous. 1972. [Review of *Sleepers Joining Hands.*] *Kirkus Reviews* 40 (15 October): 1217.

Bateson, Gregory. 1972. *Steps to an Ecology of Mind.* New York: Ballantine.

Hillman, James. 1972. *The Myth of Analysis: Three Essays in Archetypal Psychology.* New York: Harper & Row.

Lacey, Paul. 1972. *The Inner War: Forms and Themes in Recent American Poetry.* Philadelphia: Fortress Press.

Libby, Anthony. 1972. "Robert Bly Alive in Darkness." *Iowa Review* 3(3): 78-89.

Ponge, Francis. 1972. *The Voice of Things.* Translated by Beth Archer. New York: McGraw-Hill.

Cavitch, David. 1973. "Poet as Victim and Victimizer." *New York Times Book Review* (18 February): 2-3.

Chamberlin, J. E. 1973. "Poetry Chronicle." [Review of *Jumping Out of Bed.*] *Hudson Review* 26(2): 398-99.

Hall, Donald. 1973. "Notes on Robert Bly and *Sleepers Joining Hands.*" *Ohio Review* 15(1): 89-93.

Hamilton, Ian. 1973. "The Sixties Press." *A Poetry Chronicle: Essays and Reviews.* London: Faber & Faber.

Hyde, Lewis. 1973. "Let Other Poets Whisper . . . You Can Hear Bly." *Minneapolis Tribune* (25 February): 10D-11D.

Libby, Anthony. 1973. "Fire and Light, Four Poets to the End and Beyond." *Iowa Review* 4(2): 111-26.

Lindquist, Ray. 1973/74. [Review of *Sleepers Joining Hands.*] *New* 22 & 23: 88-89.

Naiden, James. 1973. "Echoes Don't Lessen Poet Bly's Strength." [Review of *Sleepers Joining Hands* and *Jumping Out of Bed.*] *Minneapolis Star* (20 November): 2 B.

Neumann, Erich. 1973. "On the Moon and Matriarchal Consciousness." In *Fathers and Mothers: Five Papers on the Archetypal Background of Family Psychology.* Translated by Hildegard Nagel. Zürich: Spring Publications.

Oates, Joyce Carol. 1973. "Where They All Are Sleeping." [Review of *Sleepers Joining Hands.*] *Modern Poetry Studies* 4(3): 341-44.

Oppenheimer, Joel. 1973. "A Newspaper Reader's Garden of Verse." [Review of *Sleepers Joining Hands.*] *Newday* (5 August): 20.

Piccione, Anthony. 1973. "Bly: Man, Voice and Poem." *Ann Arbor Review* 15-16: 86-90.

Reinhold, Robert. 1973. "The Bly Mother." [Review of *The Teeth Mother Naked at Last.*] *The Smith* 22/23: 74-79.

Skelton, Robin. 1973. "Robert Bly's New Book." [Review of *Sleepers Joining Hands.*] *Kayak* 33: 66-69.

Skinner, Knute. 1973. [Review of *The Morning Glory.*] *Concerning Poetry* 6: 89.

Sternberg, Mary. 1973. "New Work Based on Poet's Theories." *Times-Advocate* (4 February): 13.

Stitt, Peter. 1973. "James Wright and Robert Bly." [Review of *Sleepers Joining Hands* and James Wright's *Two Citizens*.] *Hawaii Review* 2: 89-94.

Walsh, Chad. 1973. "Wry Apocalypse, Revolutionary Petunias." Washington *Post Book World* (1 April): 13.

Zinnes, Harriet. 1973. "Images Plunging Inward." *New Leader* 56 (9 July): 19.

Anonymous. 1974. [Review of *Jumping Out of Bed*.] *Choice* 11: 434.

_____. 1974a. [Review of Bly's translation of *Lorca and Jiménez: Selected Poems*.] *Choice* 11: 98.

Emma, Joan E. 1974. "Letters." *American Poetry Review* 3(1): 53-54.

Irigaray, Luce. 1974. *Speculum de l'autre femme*. Paris: Editions de Minuit.

Mersmann, James. 1974. *Out of the Vietnam Vortex: A Study of Poets and Poetry Against the War*. Lawrence: University Press of Kansas.

Ramsey, Paul. 1974. "American Poetry in 1973." [Review of *Sleepers Joining Hands*.] *Sewanee Review* 82(2): 401-2.

Simpson, Louis. 1974. "Letters." *American Poetry Review* 3(1): 53.

Williamson, Alan. 1974. "Language Against Itself: The Middle Generation of Contemporary Poets." In *American Poetry Since 1960: Some Critical Perspectives*, edited by Robert B. Shaw. Chester Springs: Pa.: Dufour Editions.

Anonymous. 1975. [Review of *The Morning Glory*.] *Publishers Weekly* 208: 54.

_____. 1975a. [Review of *Old Man Rubbing His Eyes*.] *Publishers Weekly* 207: 74.

_____. 1975b. [Review of *Leaping Poetry: An Idea with Poems and Translations*.] *Kirkus Reviews* 43 (1 September): 1023-24.

Bedell, Thomas D. 1975. "Book Review." [Review of *The Morning Glory*.] *Library Journal* (1 November): 2056-57.

Capra, Fritjof. 1975. *The Tao of Physics*. Berkeley, Calif.: Shambhala Publications.

Edson, Russell. 1975. "Portrait of the Writer as a Fat Man: Some Subjective Ideas or Notions on the Care and Feeding of Prose Poems." *Field* 13: 19-29.

Fordham, Frieda. 1975. *An Introduction to Jung's Psychology*. Middlesex, Great Britain: Penguin.

Garrison, Joseph. 1975. "Book Review." [Review of *Old Man Rubbing His Eyes*.] *Library Journal* (1 April): 674.

Hillman, James. 1975. *Re-Visioning Psychology*. New York: Harper & Row.

Molesworth, Charles. 1975. "Thrashing in the Depths: The Poetry of Robert Bly." *Rocky Mountain Review of Language and Literature* 29(3-4): 95-117.

Plumly, Stanley. 1975. "Books." [Review of *The Morning Glory*.] *American Poetry Review* 4(6): 44-45.

Siemering, Bill. 1975. *Mother Consciousness*. [Videocassette recording.] (20 May) Minnesota Public Radio.

Siemering, Bill. 1975/76. "The Mother: An Interview with Robert Bly." *Dacotah Territory* 12: 30-34.

Altieri, Charles. 1976. "Gary Snyder's *Turtle Island*: The Problem of Reconciling the Roles of Seer and Prophet." *Boundary 2* 4(3): 761-77.

Anonymous. 1976. [Review of *The Morning Glory*.] *Choice* 13: 220.

_____. 1976a. [Review of *The Morning Glory*.] *Booklist* (15 April): 1162

Atkinson, Michael. 1976. "Robert Bly's *Sleepers Joining Hands*: Shadow and Self." *Iowa Review* 7(4): 135-53.

Benedikt, Michael. 1976. *The Prose Poem: An International Anthology*. New York: Dell.

Cixous, Hélène. 1976. "The Laugh of Medusa." *Signs* 1: 875-93.

Edson, Russell. 1976. "The Prose Poem in America." *Parnassus: Poetry in Review* 5(1): 321-25.

Gitzen, Julian. 1976. "Floating on Solitude: The Poetry of Robert Bly." *Modern Poetry Studies* 7(3): 231-41.

Lattimore, Richard. 1976. "Poetry Chronicle." [Review of *The Morning Glory*.] *Hudson Review* 29(1): 128-29.

Lensing, George S., and Ronald Moran. 1976. *Four Poets and the Emotive Imagination: Robert Bly, James Wright, Louis Simpson, and William Stafford*. Baton Rouge: Louisiana State University Press.

Mills, Ralph J., Jr. 1976/77. "'The Body With the Lamp Lit Inside': Robert Bly's New Poems." *Northeast* 3(2): 37-47.

Schjotz-Christensen, H. 1976. "Death and the Poet." [Review of *Old Man Rubbing His Eyes*.] *Moons and Lion Tailes* 4: 70-72.

von Franz, Marie-Louise. 1976. *The Feminine in Fairy Tales*. New York: Spring Publications.

Anonymous. 1977. [Review of *This Body Is Made of Camphor and Gopherwood*.] *Kirkus Reviews* 45: 1087.

Cooney, Seamus. 1977. "The Book Review." [Review of *Sleepers Joining Hands*.] *Library Journal* (October): 3163.

Davis, William V. 1977. "Defining the Age." [Review of *The Morning Glory*.] *Moons and Lion Tailes* 2(3): 85-89.

_____. 1977a. "Concert of One." [Unpublished Review of *This Body Is Made of Camphor and Gopherwood*].

Friberg, Ingegerd. 1977. *Moving Inward: A Study of Robert Bly's Poetry*. Göteborg, Sweden: Acta Universitatis Gothaburgensis.

Helms, Alan. 1977. "Two Poets." [Review of *Sleepers Joining Hands*.] *Partisan Review* 44(2): [284]-88.

Mersmann, James F. 1977. "Robert Bly: Rediscovering the World." [Review of *The Morning Glory*.] *Aura* 6: 40.

Rich, Adrienne. 1977. *Of Woman Born*. New York: Bantam.

Williams, Harry. 1977. *"The Edge Is What I Have:" Theodore Roethke and After*. Lewisburg, Pa.: Bucknell University Press.

Bliss, Shepherd. 1978. "Balancing Feminine and Masculine: The Mother Conference in Maine." *East/West Journal* (February): 36-39.

Breslin, Paul. 1978. "How to Read the New Contemporary Poem." *American Scholar* 47(3): 357-70.

Cotter, James Finn. 1978. "Poetry Reading." [Review of *This Body Is Made of Camphor and Gopherwood*.] *Hudson Review* 31(1): 214-15.

Dacey, Philip. 1978. "This Book Is Made of Turkey Soup and Star Music." [Review of *This Body Is Made of Camphor and Gopherwood*.] *Parnassus: Poetry in Review* 7(1): 34-45.

Daniels, Stevie, Lyndia LeMole, and Sherman Goldman. 1978. "Robert Bly on the Great Mother and the New Father." *East/West Journal* (August): 25-33.

_____. 1978a. "Robert Bly on the Great Mother and the New Father." *East/West Journal* (September): 42-46.

Dodd, Wayne. 1978. "Robert Bly: An Interview." *Ohio Review* 19(3): 32-48.

Dresbach, David. 1978. [Review of *The Morning Glory*.] *Greenfield Review* 6: 182-87.

Fass, Ekbert. 1978. "Robert Bly." In *Towards a New American Poetics: Essays and Interviews*. Santa Barbara, Calif.: Black Sparrow Press.

Fuller, John. 1978. "Where the Cold Winds Blow." [Review of *This Body Is Made of Camphor and Gopherwood*.] *Times Literary Supplement* (14 April): 410.

Hillman, James. 1978. *The Myth of Analysis: Three Essays in Archetypal Psychology*. New York: Harper Colophon.

Kenner, Hugh. 1978. "Three Poets." [Review of *This Body is Made of Camphor and Gopherwood*.] *New York Times Book Review* (1 January): 10.

M. K. S. 1978. "Books in Brief." [Review of *Old Man Rubbing His Eyes*.] *Beloit Poetry Journal* 28: 40.

Molesworth, Charles. 1978. [Review of *This Body Is Made of Camphor and Gopherwood*.] *Georgia Review* 32(3): 686-88.

_____. 1978a. "Domesticating the Sublime: Bly's Latest Poems." *Ohio Review* 19(3): 56-66.

_____. 1978b. "Contemporary Poetry and the Metaphors for the Poem." *Georgia Review* 32(2): 319-31.

Ringold, Francine. 1978. [Review of *This Body Is Made of Camphor and Gopherwood*.] *World Literature Today* 52: 471.

Saunders, William S. 1978. "Indignation Born of Love: James Wright's Ohio Poems." *Old Northwest* 4: 353-69.

Altieri, Charles. 1979. *Enlarging the Temple: New Directions in American Poetry during the 1960s*. Lewisburg, Pa.: Bucknell University Press.

Anonymous. 1979. [Review of *This Tree Will Be Here for a Thousand Years*.] *Publishers Weekly* 216: 99.

_____ 1979a. [Review of *This Tree Will Be Here for a Thousand Years*.] *Kirkus Reviews* 47: 849.

Carroll, Paul. 1979. "On Bly's Kabir." [Review of *The Kabir Book*.] *American Poetry Review* 8: 30-31.

Dacey, Philip. 1979. "The Reverend Robert E. Bly, Pastor, Church of the Blessed Unity: A Look at 'A Man Writes to a Part of Himself.'" *Pebble* 18/19/20: 1-7.

Davis, William V. 1979/80. "'Hair in a Baboon's Ear': The Politics of Robert Bly's Early Poetry." *Carleton Miscellany* 18(1): 74-84.

Garrison, Joseph. 1979. "Book Review." [Review of *This Tree Will Be Here for a Thousand Years*.] *Library Journal* (August): 1569.

Haskell, Dennis. 1979. "The Modern American Poetry of Deep Image." *Southern Review* (Australia) 12: 137-66.

Hillman, James. 1979. *The Dream and the Underworld*. New York: Harper & Row.

Molesworth, Charles. 1979. *The Fierce Embrace: A Study of Contemporary American Poetry*. Columbia: University of Missouri Press.

Weinberger, Eliot. 1979. "Gloves on a Mouse." [Review of *This Tree Will Be Here for a Thousand Years*.] *Nation* (17 November): 503-4.

Altieri, Charles. 1980. "From Experience to Discourse: American Poetry and Poetics in the Seventies." *Contemporary Literature* 21(2): 191-224.

Carruth, Hayden. 1980. "Poets on the Fringe." [Review of *This Tree Will Be Here for a Thousand Years.*] *Harper's* (January): 79.

Cotter, James Finn. 1980. "Poetry, Ego and Self." [Review of *This Tree Will Be Here for a Thousand Years.*] *Hudson Review* 33(1): 131-32.

Janik, Del Ivan. 1980. [Review of *This Tree Will Be Here for a Thousand Years.*] *Aspen Anthology* (Winter): 83-84.

Stitt, Peter. 1980. "The World at Hand." [Review of *This Tree Will Be Here for a Thousand Years.*] *Georgia Review* 34(3): 663-66.

Turner, Frederick. 1980. "'Mighty Poets in Their Misery Dead': A Polemic on the Contemporary Poetic Scene." *Missouri Review* 4(1): 77-96.

von Franz, Marie-Louise. 1980. *Shadow and Evil in Fairy Tales.* Irving, Tex.: Spring Publications.

Wilden, Anthony. 1980. *System and Structure: Essays in Communication and Exchange.* 2ᵈ ed. New York: Tavistock.

Williamson, Alan. 1980. "Music to Your Ears." [Review of *This Tree Will Be Here for a Thousand Years.*] *New York Times Book Review* (9 March): 8-9, 14-15.

Agee, Joel. 1981. "Pony or Pegasus." [Review of *Selected Poems of Rainer Maria Rilke.*] *Harper's* 263 (September): 70-72.

Anonymous. 1981. [Review of *The Man in the Black Coat Turns.*] *Publishers Weekly* 220: 48.

Berman, Morris. 1981. *The Reenchantment of the World.* Ithaca, N.Y.: Cornell University Press.

Davis, William V. 1981. "'At the Edges of the Light': A Reading of Robert Bly's *Sleepers Joining Hands.*" *Poetry East* 4/5: 265-82.

Haines, John. 1981. "Robert Bly: A Tiny Retrospect." *Poetry East* 4/5: 190-93.

Hall, Donald. 1981. "Poetry Food." *Poetry East* 4/5: 35-36.

Harris, Victoria Frenkel. 1981. "'Walking Where the Plows have Been Turning': Robert Bly and Female Consciousness." *Poetry East* 4/5: 123-38.

_____. 1981a. "Criticism and the Incorporative Consciousness." *Centennial Review* 25(4): 417-34.

Jones, Richard, and Kate Daniels. 1981. *Of Solitude and Silence: Writings on Robert Bly*. Boston: Beacon Press.

Libby, Anthony. 1981. "Dreaming of Animals." *Plainsong* 3(2): 47-54.

Mills, Ralph J., Jr. 1981. "'Of Energy Compacted and Whirling': Robert Bly's Recent Prose Poems." *New Mexico Humanities Review* 4(2): 29-49.

Nelson, Cary. 1981. *Our Last First Poets: Vision and History in Contemporary American Poetry*. Urbana: University of Illinois Press.

Orr, Gregory. 1981. "The Need for Poetics: Some Thoughts on Robert Bly." *Poetry East* 4/5: 116-22.

Roffman, Rosaly DeMaios. 1981. "Book Review." [Review of *The Man in the Black Coat Turns*.] *Library Journal* 106: 2032.

Rolf, Fjelde. 1981. "Poems as Meeting Places." [Review of Bly's translation of Tomas Tranströmer's *Truth Barriers*.] *New York Times Book Review* (26 April): 26.

Saucerman, James R. 1981. [Review of *This Tree Will Be Here For a Thousand Years*.] *Western American Literature* 16(2): 162-64.

Seal, David. 1981. "Waking to 'Sleepers Joining Hands'." *Poetry East* 4/5: 234-63.

Turner, Frederick. 1981-82. "Response to Mr. Bly." *Missouri Review* 5(2): 196-98.

von Franz, Marie-Louise. 1981. *Puer Aeternus*. Boston: Sigo Press.

Wesling, Donald. 1981. "The Recent Work of Donald Hall and Robert Bly." [Review essay of *This Tree Will Be Here for a Thousand Years* and *Talking All Morning*.] *Michigan Quarterly Review* 20(2): 144-54.

_____. 1981a. "The Wisdom-Writer." [Review of *The Man in the Black Coat Turns*.] *Nation* (31 October): 447-48.

Zavatsky, Bill. 1981. "Talking Back: A Response to Robert Bly." *Poetry East* 4/5: 86-98.

Anonymous. 1982. [Review of *The Man in the Black Coat Turns*.] *Booklist* (1 January): 582.

Capra, Fritjof. 1982. *The Turning Point: Science, Society, and the Rising Culture*. New York: Simon and Schuster.

Davis, William V. 1982. "'Camphor and Gopherwood': Robert Bly's Recent Poems in Prose." *Modern Poetry Studies* 11(1&2): 88-102.

_____. 1982a. "'Still the Place Where Creation Does Some Work on Itself': Robert Bly's Most Recent Work." In *Robert Bly: When Sleepers Awake*, edited by Joyce Peseroff (1984). Ann Arbor: University of Michigan Press.

Jarman, Mark. 1982. "The Poetry of Non Sequitur: *The Man in the Black Coat Turns*." *American Book Review* 4(4): 13-14.

Hass, Robert. 1982. "Looking for Rilke." In *The Selected Poetry of Rainer Maria Rilke*, edited by Stephen Mitchell. New York: Random House.

Heller, Erich. 1982. "On Translating Lyric Poetry." [Review of *Selected Poems of Rainer Maria Rilke*.] *New Republic* (3 March): 27-31.

Molesworth, Charles. 1982. [Review of *The Man in the Black Coat Turns*.] *Western American Literature* 17(3): 282-84.

Perloff, Marjorie. 1982. "Soft Touch." [Review of *The Man in the Black Coat Turns*.] *Parnassus: Poetry in Review* 10(1): 209-30.

Peters, Robert. 1982. "News from Robert Bly's Universe: *The Man in the Black Coat Turns*." In *Robert Bly: When Sleepers Awake*, edited by Joyce Peseroff (1984). Ann Arbor: University of Michigan Press.

Shakarchi, Joseph. 1982. "An Interview with Robert Bly." *Massachusetts Review* 23(2): 226-43.

Stitt, Peter. 1982. "Dark Volumes." [Review of *The Man in the Black Coat Turns*.] *New York Times Book Review* (14 February): 15, 37.

Stuewe, Paul. 1982. [Review of *The Man In the Black Coat Turns*.] *Quill &*
Quire 48: 39.

Thompson, Keith. 1982. "What Men Really Want." *New Age Journal* (7 May):
30-37, 50-51.

Crowder, Dianne Griffin. 1983. "Amazons and Mothers: Monique Wittig,
Hélène Cixous and Theories of Women's Writing." *Contemporary*
Literature 24(2): 117-44.

Fredman, Stephen. 1983. *Poet's Prose: The Crisis in American Verse.*
Cambridge, Great Britain: Cambridge University Press.

Holden, Jonathan. 1983. "Postmodern Poetic Form: A Theory." *New England*
Review and Bread Loaf Quarterly 6(1): 1-22.

Kramer, Lawrence. 1983. "A Sensible Emptiness: Robert Bly and the Poetics
of Immanence." *Contemporary Literature* 24(4): 448-61.

Miller, Brown. 1983. "Searching for Poetry: Real vs. Fake." [Review of *The*
Man in the Black Coat Turns.] *San Francisco Review of Books* (8 July): 22.

Reynolds, Michael S. 1983. [Review of *The Man in the Black Coat Turns*.] In
Magill's Literary Annual 1983, edited by Frank N. Magill. Englewood
Cliffs, N.J.: Salem Press.

Breslin, James E. B. 1984. *From Modern to Contemporary: American Poetry,*
1945-65. Chicago: University of Chicago Press.

Davis, William V. 1984. "'In a Low Voice to Someone He is Sure is
Listening': Robert Bly's Recent Poems in Prose." *Midwest Quarterly*
25(2): 148-56.

Libby, Anthony. 1984. *Mythologies of Nothing: Mystical Death in American*
Poetry 1940-70. Urbana: University of Illinois Press.

Nelson, Howard. 1984. *Robert Bly: An Introduction to the Poetry.* New York:
Columbia University Press.

Peseroff, Joyce. 1984. *Robert Bly: When Sleepers Awake.* Ann Arbor: University
of Michigan Press.

Thompson, Keith. 1984. "Robert Bly on Fathers and Sons." *Esquire* (April):
238-39.

Unterecker, John. 1984. "Foreword" to *Robert Bly: An Introduction to the Poetry*, by Howard Nelson. New York: Columbia University Press.

Brumer, Andy. 1985. "Loving as the Bridge." [Review of *Loving a Woman in Two Worlds*.] *Poetry Flash* 152: 1, 6.

Chappell, Fred. 1985. "Sepia Photographs and Jazz Solos." [Review of *Loving a Woman in Two Worlds*.] *New York Times Book Review* (13 October): 15.

Emery, Edward J. 1985. "Bly's Poetics." [Letter to the Editor.] *New York Times Book Review* (17 November): 42.

Harris, Victoria Frenkel. 1985. "Relationship and Change: Text and Context of James Wright's 'Blue Teal's Mother' and Robert Bly's 'With Pale Women in Maryland'." *American Poetry* 3(1): 43-56.

Irigarey, Luce. 1985. *This Sex Which Is Not One*. (Translated by Catherine Porter.) Ithaca: Cornell University Press.

Lauter, Estella, and Carol Schreier Rupprecht, editors. 1985. *Feminist Archetypal Theory: Interdisciplinary Re-Visions of Jungian Thought*. Knoxville: University of Tennessee Press.

Lehman, David. 1985. "The Prosaic Principle." [Review of *The Man in the Black Coat Turns*.] *Partisan Review* 52(3): 302-4.

Myers, Jack, and Michael Simms. 1985. *Longman Dictionary and Handbook of Poetry*. White Plains, N.Y.: Longman.

Stuewe, Paul, 1985. [Review of *Loving a Woman in Two Worlds*.] *Quill & Quire* 51: 29.

Sugg, Richard P. 1985. "Robert Bly and the Poetics of Evolutionary Psychology." *Journal of Evolutionary Psychology* 6(1-2): 33-37.

Anonymous. 1986. "Notes on Current Books." [Review of *Loving a Woman in Two Worlds*.] *Virginia Quarterly Review* 62(1): 27.

Dacey, Philip. 1986. "Saint Robert." [Review of *Loving a Woman in Two Worlds*.] *American Book Review* 8: 13-14.

Kakutani, Michiko. 1986. [Review of *Selected Poems*.] *New York Times* (3 May): 15.

Peseroff, Joyce. 1986. "Minnesota Transcendentalist." [Review of *Selected Poems*.] *New York Times Book Review* (25 May): 2.

Richman, Robert. 1986. "The Poetry of Robert Bly." *The New Criterion* 5(4): 37-46.

Roberson, William H. 1986. *Robert Bly: A Primary and Secondary Bibliography*. Metuchen, N. J.: Scarecrow Press.

Smith, Laurel, and Robert E. Taylor. 1986. "Moving with the Deep Image in the Poetry of Robert Bly." *Journal of Mental Imagery* 10(2): 113-19.

Stitt, Peter. 1986. "Coherence Through Place in Contemporary American Poetry." [Review of *Selected Poems*.] *Georgia Review* 40(4): 1021-33.

Sugg, Richard P. 1986. *Robert Bly*. Boston: Twayne.

Ardinger, Richard. 1987. [Review of *Selected Poems*.] *Western American Literature* 22(1): 95.

Bliss, Shepherd. 1987. "The Men of the Wound." In *New Men, New Minds: Breaking Male Tradition*, edited by Franklin Abbott. Freedom, Calif.: Crossing Press.

Gioia, Dana. 1987. "The Successful Career of Robert Bly." *Hudson Review* 40(2): 207-23.

Hamill, Sam. 1987. "Lyric, Miserable Lyric (Or: Whose Dog Are You?)." [Review of *Loving a Woman in Two Worlds*.] *American Poetry Review* 16(5): 31.

LeClair, Tom. 1987. *In the Loop: Don DeLillo and the Systems Novel*. Urbana: University of Illinois Press.

Lovelock, J. E. 1987. *Gaia: A New Look at Life on Earth*. New York: Oxford University Press.

Monroe, Jonathan. 1987. *A Poverty of Objects: The Prose Poem and the Politics of Genre*. Ithaca, N.Y.: Cornell University Press.

Perkins, David. 1987. *A History of Modern Poetry: Modernism and After*. Cambridge: Harvard University Press.

Raksin, Alex. 1987. [Review of *Loving a Woman in Two Worlds.*] *Los Angeles Book Review* (22 February): 10.

Young, David. 1987. "The Naturalizing of Surrealism." [Review of *Selected Poems.*] *Field* 36: 90-94.

Davis, William V. 1988. *Understanding Robert Bly.* Columbia: University of South Carolina Press.

Melnyczuk, Askold. 1988. "Robert Bly" [Review of *Selected Poems.*] *Partisan Review* 65(1): 167-71.

Mitchell, Roger. 1988. "Robert Bly and the Trouble with American Poetry." *Ohio Review* 42: 86-92.

Harris, Victoria Frenkel. 1989. "Scribe, Inscription, Inscribed: Sexuality in the Poetry of Robert Bly and Adrienne Rich." In *Discontented Discourses: Feminism/Textual Intervention/ Psychoanalysis*, edited by Marleen S. Barr and Richard Feldsteins. Urbana: University of Illinois Press.

Kalaidjian, Walter. 1989. *Languages of Liberation: The Social Text in Contemporary American Poetry.* New York: Columbia University Press.

Rutsala, Vern. 1989. *"Déjà Vu*: Thoughts on the Fifties and Eighties." *American Poetry Review* 18: 29-35.

Abrams, William. 1990. [Review of *Iron John: A Book About Men.*] *Library Journal* (15 November): 83.

Appelbaum, David. 1990. "Not at Home: The Search for the Father." *Parabola* 15(3): 98-104, 124-25.

Brumer, Andy. 1990. "Bly looks into the heart of man." [Review of *Iron John: A Book About Men.*] *Los Angeles Daily News* (30 December): 29.

Csikszentmihalyi, Mihaly. 1990. "Bring on the Hairy Mentor." [Review of *Iron John: A Book About Men.*] *New York Times Book Review* (9 December): 15-16.

Gross, Daniel. 1990. "The Gender Rap." *New Republic* (16 April): 11-14.

Harris, Victoria Frenkel. 1990. "'Walking Swiftly' with Freedom: Robert Bly's Prose Poems." *American Poetry* 7(2): 13-30.

_____. 1990a. "A Systems Approach to Robert Bly's *This Tree Will Be Here for a Thousand Years*. In *Germany and German Thought in American Literature and Cultural Criticism: Proceedings of the German-American Conference in Paderborn, May 16-18, 1990,* edited by Peter Freese. Essen, Germany: *Die Blaue Eule*: 433-53.

Moore, Robert, and Douglas Gillette. 1990. *King Warrior Magician Lover: Rediscovering the Archetypes of the Mature Masculine*. New York: HarperSanFrancisco.

Wagenheim, Jeff. 1990. "The Secret Life of Men." *New Age Journal* (October): 40-45, 106-13.

Allen, Charlotte. 1991. "The Little Prince." [Review of *Iron John: A Book About Men*.] *Commentary* 91(5): 58-60.

Appelo, Tim. 1991. "The Bly Guys." *Entertainment Weekly* (19 April): 23-24.

Eckhoff, Sally S. 1991. [Review of *Iron John: A Book About Men*.] *Voice Literary Supplement* 92: 8.

Faludi, Susan. 1991. *Backlash: The Undeclared War Against American Women*. New York: Crown.

Garvey, Michael O. 1991. [Review of *Iron John: A Book About Men*.] *Books & Religion* 18: 5.

Kuusisto, Stephen. 1991. "Robert Bly's *Iron John* and the New 'Lawrentian' Man." *Seneca Review* 21(1): 77-86.

Lammon, Martin. 1991. "A Sustained Raid into Modern Life: The Critical Commentary of Robert Bly, 1958-1986." Ph.D. dissertation, Ohio University.

_____. 1991a. "A Sustained Raid into Modern Life: The Critical Commentary of Robert Bly, 1958-1986." *Dissertation Abstracts International* 52(5): 1743-44.

Levine, Art. 1991. "Masculinity's Champion." *U.S. News & World Report* (8 April): 61-62.

Morrison, Blake. 1991. [Review of *Iron John: A Book About Men*.] *Times Literary Supplement* (27 September): 36.

Morrow, Lance. 1991. "The Child Is Father of the Man." *Time* (19 August): 52-54.

Neafsey, James. 1991. "Real Quiche." [Review of *Iron John: A Book About Men.*] *Commonweal* (3 May): 299.

Schmidt, Stephen A. 1991. "Recovering the Wild Man." *Christian Century* (29 May-5 June): 591-93.

Smith, R. W. 1991. [Review of *Iron John: A Book About Men.*] *Choice* 28(7): 1234.

Solotaroff, Ted. 1991. "Captain Bly." *Nation* (9 September): 270-74.

Tacey, David J. 1991. "Attacking Patriarchy, Redeeming Masculinity." *San Francisco Jung Institute Library Journal* 10: 25-41.

Warren, Catherine. 1991. "Myths Make the Man." [Review of *Iron John: A Book About Men.*] *New Statesman and Society* (27 September): 54.

Allen, Danielle. 1992. [Review of *What Have I Ever Lost by Dying?*] *National Review* 44(14): 50.

Anonymous. 1992. [Review of *What Have I Ever Lost by Dying?*] *Publishers Weekly* 239: 17.

_____. 1992a. "Where Are Women and Men Today? Robert Bly and Deborah Tannen in Conversation." *New Age Journal* (February): 28-33, 92-97.

Briggs, Joe Bob. 1992. "Get in Touch With Your Ancient Spear: A Manly Seminar With Iron Joe Bob." *New York Times Book Review* (31 May): 44-45.

Davis, William V. 1992. *Critical Essays on Robert Bly.* New York: G. K. Hall.

_____. 1992a. "The Teeth Mother Naked at Last." In *Masterplots II: Poetry,* edited by Frank N. Magill. Pasadena, Calif.: Salem Press.

_____. 1992b. "Robert Bly." In *Critical Survey of Poetry: English Language Series,* revised edition, edited by Frank N. Magill. Pasadena: Calif.: Salem Press.

Dodd, Wayne. 1992. "Back to the Snowy Fields." In *Critical Essays on Robert Bly,* edited by William V. Davis. New York: G. K. Hall.

Estés, Clarissa Pinkola. 1992. *Women Who Run with the Wolves: Myths and Stories of the Wild Woman Archetype*. New York: Ballantine.

Galin, Saul. 1992. "The Third Male." In *Walking Swiftly: Writings & Images on the Occasion of Robert Bly's 65th Birthday*, edited by Thomas R. Smith. St. Paul, Minn.: Ally Press.

Hall, Donald. 1992. "Young Bly." In *Critical Essays on Robert Bly*, edited by William V. Davis. New York: G. K. Hall.

Hansen, Tom. 1992. "Robert Bly's *Iron John*." *Literary Review* 35(3): 415-18.

Harris Victoria Frenkel. 1992. *The Incorporative Consciousness of Robert Bly*. Carbondale: Southern Illinois University Press.

_____ 1992a. "Received from Robert Bly: Two Lessons and a Message." In *Walking Swiftly: Writings & Images on the Occasion of Robert Bly's 65th Birthday*, edited by Thomas R. Smith. St. Paul, Minn.: Ally Press.

Johnson, Diane. 1992. "Something for the Boys." [Review of *Iron John: A Book About Men*.] *New York Review of Books* (16 January): 13-17.

Johnston, Jill. 1992. "Why Iron John Is No Gift to Women." *New York Times Book Review* (23 February): 1, 28-31, 33.

Kimmel, Michael S. 1992. "Reading Men: Men, Masculinity, and Publishing." *Contemporary Sociology* 21(2): 162-71.

Moore, Robert L. 1992. "Robert Bly and True Greatness: Some Musings from the Study of Leadership in Human Culture." In *Walking Swiftly: Writings & Images on the Occasion of Robert Bly's 65th Birthday*, edited by Thomas R. Smith. St. Paul, Minn.: Ally Press.

Myers, George, Jr. 1992. "'Iron John': An Interview with Robert Bly." *Literary Review* 35(3): 408-14.

Poole, Francis. 1992. [Review of *What Have I Ever Lost by Dying?*] *Library Journal* (1 June): 10.

Rehder, Robert. 1992. "Which Way to the Future?" In *Critical Essays On Robert Bly*, edited by William V. Davis. New York: G. K. Hall.

Ross, Andrew. 1992. "Wet, Dark, and Low, Eco-Man Evolves from Eco-Woman." *Boundary 2* 19(2): 205-32.

Seaman, Donna. 1992. [Review of *What Have I Ever Lost by Dying?*] *Booklist* (1 May): 17.

Seyfarth, Susan. 1992. "Arnold Schwarzenegger and *Iron John*: Predator to Protector." *Studies in Popular Culture* 15(1): 75-81.

Smith, Thomas R., editor. 1992. *Walking Swiftly: Writings & Images on the Occasion of Robert Bly's 65th Birthday*. St. Paul, Minn.: Ally Press.

Stitt, Peter. 1992. "The Startling Journeys of Robert Bly." In *Critical Essays on Robert Bly*, edited by William V. Davis. New York: G. K. Hall.

True, Michael. 1992. "Celebrating Robert Bly, but Taking Him to Task as Well." In *Walking Swiftly: Writings & Images on the Occasion of Robert Bly's 65th Birthday*, edited by Thomas R. Smith. St. Paul, Minn.: Ally Press.

Udovitch, Mim. 1992. [Interview with Robert Bly.] *Mirabelle* (October): 36.

Ventura, Michael. 1992. "An Open Letter to Robert Bly on His Sixty-fifth Birthday." In *Walking Swiftly: Writings & Images on the Occasion of Robert Bly's 65th Birthday*, edited by Thomas R. Smith. St. Paul, Minn.: Ally Press.

Weissman, Judith. 1992. "A Woman's View of *Iron John*." In *Walking Swiftly: Writings & Images on the Occasion of Robert Bly's 65th Birthday*, edited by Thomas R. Smith. St. Paul, Minn.: Ally Press.

Ziegenhals, Gretchen E. 1992. "Hairy Christians for Bly." *The Christian Century* (29 July-5 August): 700-2.

Zipes, Jack. 1992. "Spreading Myths about Fairy Tales: A Critical Commentary on Robert Bly's *Iron John*." *New German Critique: An Interdisciplinary Journal of German Studies* 55: 3-19.

Chang, Leslie C. 1993. [Review of *What Have I Ever Lost by Dying?*] *Harvard Review* 3: 187-88.

Heller, Scott. 1993. "Disconcerted by the 'Iron John' Movement, Many Scholars Call It Simplistic." *Chronicle of Higher Education* (3 February): A8.

Howard, Jerry, and Jeff Wagenheim. 1993. "Men on Midlife: Straight Talk About Women, Power, Money, God, and the Myth of the Midlife Crisis." *New Age Journal* (July/August): 53, 55-56.

Kakutani, Michiko. 1993. "Beyond Iron John? How About Iron Jane?" *New York Times* (27 August): C1, C28.

Lense, Edward. 1993. "A Voice for the Wild Man: Robert Bly and the Rhetoric of Public Poetry." *AWP Chronicle* 26(2): 17-20.

Wiliamson, Marianne. 1993. *A Woman's Worth*. New York: Random House.

Index